L. Perry Wilbur is an advertising consultant and author of seven books and thousands of articles.
Frank S. Caprio, M.D., is director of the Florida Association for Self-Improvement and has written thirty-three books.

L. Perry Wilbur

Frank S. Caprio, M.D.

HOW TO ENJOY YOURSELF

The Antidote Book
for Unhappiness and Depression

A SPECTRUM BOOK

Prentice-Hall, Inc., Englewood Cliffs, N.J. 07632

Library of Congress Cataloging in Publication Data

Wilbur, L. Perry.
  How to enjoy yourself.

  "A Spectrum book."
  Includes index.
    1. Happiness. 2. Depression, Mental. I. Caprio,
Frank Samuel, 1906– . II. Title.
BF575.H27W54   158'.1   82-7556
                         AACR2

ISBN 0-13-405688-4 {PBK}

ISBN 0-13-405696-5

ACKNOWLEDGMENT
Page 142, from an article by Michael Korda, "Pleasure: How to Let Your Senses Rip,"
published in *Self Magazine*.

This Spectrum Book is available to businesses and organizations at a special discount
when ordered in large quantities. For information, contact Prentice-Hall, Inc., General
Publishing Division, Special Sales, Englewood Cliffs, N.J. 07632.

A SPECTRUM BOOK

10 9 8 7 6 5 4 3 2 1

Printed in the United States of America

Editorial/production supervision and interior design by Publication Arts, Hawthorne, N.J.
Cover design by Jeannette Jacobs
Manufacturing buyer: Cathie Lenard

Prentice-Hall International, Inc., *London*
Prentice-Hall of Australia Pty., Limited, *Sydney*
Prentice-Hall Canada Inc., *Toronto*
Prentice-Hall of India Private, Limited, *New Delhi*
Prentice-Hall of Japan, Inc., *Tokyo*
Prentice-Hall of Southeast Asia Pte., Ltd., *Singapore*
Whitehall Books Limited, *Wellington, New Zealand*

Dedicated to Our Readers

With the hope that this book may provide you with
the key to a successful and more enjoyable way of life.

Contents

Foreword

As a psychiatrist for over thirty-seven years, I have encountered innumerable examples of successful men and women who were unhappy. They obviously never learned to enjoy themselves.

I recall the case of a married college professor who had been a serious-minded, hard-working scholar practically all of his life. Up to his forty-fifth year he had shown no interest in pleasures and pastimes; then, suddenly he experienced a transformation of personality. He developed a zest for life, enjoyed his daily happy hour martini, attended plays, took up golf, made new friends and signed up for dancing lessons.

His anxious wife requested a psychiatric examination because of this sudden change in her husband's behavior. It was determined that our friend was merely experiencing a delayed youth, making up for the good times he had missed. His own justification was that he found himself and that he was just beginning to live.

This is an entirely human and, in some respects, even a commendable reaction. Such tardy awakening of the normal instinct for self-enjoyment can be interpreted as an *antidote* to feelings of "burnout," unhappiness and depression experienced by many successful people today. We have even begun to speak of a "Burnout Syndrome."

In another instance, I encountered the case of a widow of a millionaire who had been referred to me for counseling because of her "feelings of weariness, self-discontent, loneliness associated with boredom and lack of interest in everything." Her doctor informed me that she was in good physical health, but she was never able to adjust emotionally following the death of her beloved husband—another example of unhappiness and depression. She stated that she felt only half-alive and was obsessed with the idea that she would never be happy.

I explained to her that to be unhappy temporarily, under the circumstances, was a normal reaction, but to *remain unhappy* indefinitely is abnormal—that chronic unhappiness is an illness of the mind.

Incidentally, many widows become victims of chronic unhappiness. They hug their grief to their breasts for fear they will forget. They keep reminding themselves of their misfortunes. They verbalize their unhappiness by telling their friends about their battle with loneliness.

Loneliness is self-created. It's a form of sugar-coated self-pity. When our friend realized she was afraid to be happy, subconsciously reluctant to enjoy herself, she agreed to assume a new lease on life. She took a more joyous attitude toward life.

Despite the advantage of being financially independent and secure, she suffered from *emotional* insecurity. Her self-image was a negative one. She had lost her self-esteem. She was made to understand that first she had to love herself to enjoy herself.

Love of oneself and love of life itself is the best antidote for unhappiness. The enjoyment of oneself begins with inner content—*self-happiness*. It starts with the premise that happiness is a state of mind— that life can be beautiful at any age and more important, that *life is to be enjoyed*, as demonstrated throughout this book.

Each morning when you awake should not be just another day. It is in fact a new beginning—a new opportunity to make each day a good day—to add life to your years and not merely years to your life.

Every day should be a new passion for living—a new day to enjoy the fruits of life that you so richly deserve—a new day to learn and accomplish what you set out to do. You can generate a determined resolution to live today, tomorrow and every day with a positive attitude toward yourself and life. Self-love is indispensable to enjoying yourself.

You can become a casualty of life's sorrows and misfortunes or survive the symptom-consequences of the Burnout Syndrome and *enjoy yourself*. The choice is yours.

It is my sincere hope that with your willingness to utilize the information contained in this book, you will experience a new dimension to life—a healthier and more enjoyable lifestyle based on your right to enjoy yourself.

Frank S. Caprio, M.D.

If we are ever to enjoy life, now is the time—not tomorrow, nor next year, nor in some future life after we have died. The best preparation for a better life next year is a full, complete harmonious, joyous life this year. Our beliefs in a rich future life are of little importance unless we coin them into a rich present life. Today should always be our most wonderful day. . .

Thomas Drier

NOTE:
The "I" making comments throughout this book is me, L. Perry Wilbur. Although the point of view is often first-person singular, be assured that Dr. Caprio has been looking over my shoulder throughout, and the book is as much his as mine.

1

Don't Be Afraid
to Be Happy

Are you afraid to be happy? Are you afraid to enjoy yourself? Unfortunately, these descriptive phrases are true of many people all over the globe. You may know of someone (perhaps a family member, relative, friend, associate or neighbor) who has such a fear. It is a widespread one. This book is meant to be an antidote for anyone who is afraid to be happy and enjoy life. There's a world of enjoyment out there, and the pages of this book may open it up to you.

Many individuals who are afraid to be happy and are unable to enjoy themselves seek the help of psychiatrists. Their tensions often come from a fear of relaxing. They seldom allow themselves to smile, and many of them keep reliving an unhappy past. Usually they were conditioned to expect unhappiness in childhood and the pattern of inhibitions persists to adulthood, preventing them from taking pleasure in life when it has become available. The feelings of social inadequacy and inferiority that they develop make them withdraw into a shell.

As an example, one patient even reached the point of fearing that, in his depression, he might do himself an injury. "I feel utterly discouraged," he said. "I don't seem to be able to cultivate any worthwhile friendships with women. It's my fault, because I never learned to dance. All through my adolescence I was extremely shy and self-conscious. My parents are partly to blame. They were always quarreling over money matters. You see, we were very poor. My sister and I were taught that it was extravagant to spend money for the movies or for candy or other pleasures. We never learned to enjoy ourselves."

The patient continued. "When I was fifteen, I told my mother I was going to run away. I blamed her for my not having had an education. I have always felt guilty over that, and I've been trying to make up for it by sacrificing personal pleasures in order to send her money regularly. I want to be a good son and never hurt her again. She writes back and tells me she doesn't need money. But if I didn't send it, I'd only put it in the bank, because I can't bear to spend it on pleasure. If I go to a party, I'm too inhibited to have a good time. I lead a very lonesome existence. Actually, I'm afraid to enjoy myself. I'm responsible for my own unhappiness."

His story is typical of many individuals who come from homes where pleasures were restricted. They have been conditioned to "all work and no play" and are unable to grow out of the habits of self-deprivation.

There are others who have been afraid to be happy. Elizabeth Barrett would most likely have lived the rest of her life as an invalid, if British poet Robert Browning hadn't come into her life. Elizabeth was certainly afraid to be happy, mainly because of the dominating selfishness of her tyrannical father. He dictated her daily life, in his determination to keep her at home with him always.

But after Robert Browning met and quickly grew to love Elizabeth, he changed the face of all the world for her. He brought new joy into her sick world and taught her how wrong she was to be afraid to be happy. Her love for Robert gave her the strength to elope with him. And in so doing, she saved her own life and found a whole new world of joy, contentment, and meaning.

MANY BELIEVE THEY HAVE NO RIGHT TO BE HAPPY

There are persons from all walks of life who really believe that it's wrong to be happy or to express happiness. Many of these individuals suffer from a guilt syndrome, which causes them to embrace this attitude. They tell themselves that God hasn't forgiven them for some transgression. Since they don't believe that God has forgiven them, they don't forgive themselves.

Still others have convinced themselves that it's somehow wrong to be happy, that if they admit to being happy something terrible will happen to them, or some awful event will take place in their lives.

Superstition may be a cause of unhappiness. Perhaps a series of misfortunes or tragedies has helped to shape such a viewpoint. A statement once made about the Kennedy family comes to mind here: "The Kennedy family has always been jinxed by wealth." Here is a clear example of superstition.

Howard Hughes and Elvis Presley

In his last known public communication, billionaire Howard Hughes made a revealing statement on national television (via a telephone hookup): "I'm an unhappy man." With a fortune estimated at from $180 million to over $2 billion, Hughes lived like a recluse, suffered from a number of phobias, and feared most of his life that people were out to get his money. His strange lifestyle eventually did him in.

Elvis Presley may also have been afraid to be happy simply because his lifestyle, like that of Hughes, prevented it. What good were their fortunes when they couldn't go and come as they pleased like normal human beings? They paid an enormous personal price for their fortunes; both of them gave up their own freedom. Elvis was also afraid of being attacked or shot during a live on-stage performance.

Examples of Not Being Afraid to Be Happy

Children aren't afraid to be happy. Happiness just comes naturally for most of them. I remember visiting my sister and her family in Virginia a few years ago. My two nephews were eight and six years old at the time. Every morning bright and early at 5:30, I would hear two young voices talking to me. Upon opening my eyes, there stood my two smiling nephews Gavin and Andrew beside my bed. "Get up, Uncle Perry, it's morning!" If I tried to turn over and go back to sleep, after greeting them both, they would continue to talk to me and urge me to rise and shine. In their view, it was another wonderful day to be happy, and they were eager to get on with it.

I also remember two neighbors, both sisters, who lived together in Indiana for many years. Neither sister ever married. They lived around the corner from my family, when we lived in Nappanee, a small town about thirty miles south of South Bend, Indiana.

One of the sisters, Daisy, loved to work in the large garden behind her house. Her garden was her pride and joy. I was about seven years old at the time, and I loved both of these sisters whose last name was Gray. I especially liked Daisy and made sure that all the other children in the neighborhood stayed out of her garden. I knew how much she cared about it.

The Gray sisters may have both been spinsters, but they certainly didn't let it keep them from being happy. They got more out of life than many others in the area. They were in on all the town's parties and social events, active in school, church, and civic affairs, and visited their friends and neighbors often. Every day was a happy experience for them.

The great highlight of the lives of the Gray sisters came when they spent a winter in Florida, met the noted film producer Cecil B. DeMille, and were invited to be extras in DeMille's circus film "The Greatest Show on Earth," which was then shooting in Florida. They got more enjoyment from being in that movie than anything else in their lives. After the film was completed, they returned to Indiana and told all their friends about their unforgettable experience. They never forgot it and got pleasure from the happy memories of that summer for many years to come.

The Gray sisters knew how to *enjoy* each new day. They weren't afraid to be happy. Today, many years later, whenever I think of them, it's their happy natures I remember most and their capacity for enjoyment. They knew the secret of living—that you have to make your own happiness. And they expressed their happiness on a daily basis.

My own grandmother lost her husband, son, and the lovely home she had in Tennessee. For the rest of her life, she alternated living with her two daughters, spending a year with one daughter in Texas and the next year with her other daughter in Memphis, Tennessee. She refused to be unhappy over what had happened.

She enjoyed writing to all her friends and grandchildren so much and sending them little gifts. She centered her life around the wisdom of the basic proverbs and was called "the Proverb Lady" by her grandchildren. She was not afraid to be happy.

Look at the enjoyment of entertaining audiences, derived by stars like Bob Hope, Joan Rivers, Phyllis Diller, Milton Berle, and many others. I believe that many of them would continue to entertain others, whether they received payment or not. What's in it for them shows on their faces, and that is pure enjoyment.

President Ronald Reagan takes time to be happy and to enjoy himself. Despite the demands on his time and the long days he puts in, he gets in some time at his ranch with his horses. Time spent at his ranch gives him a better perspective on everything that happens. "You'd be surprised how much clear thinking you can do on horseback." Reagan has only the last ten minutes of the day to devote to reading. "It takes me a long time to read a book. I've finished a book on Roosevelt, I've finished a book on Lincoln and I'm now into a novel. And I have another book on Peter the Great up at Camp David—and that one is going to take an awful long time."

DON'T POSTPONE YOUR HAPPINESS

Many patients have told Dr. Caprio they can't be happy until they get that new home, or have a certain amount of money in the bank, a new 450SL Mercedes Benz, or have put the last kid through college, or what have you. It's a lot smarter to be as happy as you can *today*, now, with what you have.

You've heard it before, but it's well worth repeating. Don't live in the future or in the past. The only chance you have to be happy is to take each day as it comes, do your best, and make up your mind to be as happy as possible. Live in the present. "Relish the moment" is a good motto. Yesterday is gone forever, and tomorrow may never come. The only thing you have and can be sure of is today. So make the most of it. Here are some guidelines to help you be a happier person each day:

- Take the advice of David Hartman, the genial host of "Good Morning, America." "Go out and make it a good day." You can do even more. Make today the *best day* of your life.

- You must enjoy yourself, before you can find enjoyment in life.
- Unhappiness is an illness.
- Today is now. Tomorrow is another idea. Don't postpone love. Don't postpone happiness. Don't postpone enjoyment.
- Wake up and enjoy life. One purpose of life is to enjoy everything.

Happiness: The capacity to enjoy yourself stems from the conviction that happiness is a state of mind that can be cultivated.

Laughter: Laughter is essential to normal living as oxygen is to the lungs. It is an antidote for the day-to-day frustrations that can destroy a healthy mind. Laughter lifts the emotional strain which many feel. It thrusts aside gloomy thoughts.

Unhappiness: If you are at odds with yourself, you can't expect to enjoy yourself or life itself. If you are fighting your world, business or family, look to yourself for the origins of your discontent. Until you learn the cause of your own private unhappiness, you cannot expect to find life enjoyable. While there is war within yourself, there can be no peace for those who want to associate or live with you.

If you feel depressed and anxious most of the time, you should consult your family physician or ask him to refer you to a psychiatrist. It is especially important to seek psychiatric help right away if you find yourself frequently thinking about suicide. Professional counseling and treatment with new medicines can eliminate depression and anxiety in many cases or make life seem much brighter.

Love: There is a simple but profound truth in this statement: "Love comes from making others happy." An altruistic attitude toward life will improve your chances of enjoying life. Love is a condition of the mind, a sense of inner tranquility that communicates itself to others.

Life: Life is like a pair of scales, delicately balanced, dipping first to one side and then to the other as new weight is added. The well-adjusted person will keep the balance even.

Don't let the painful realities of life overbalance appreciation of its beauty and joyousness.

Relaxation: Many persons find it difficult to enjoy themselves, because they have never learned to *relax*. They are in constant tension, afraid to relax and seldom allow themselves to smile. They spend much of their time living in the past. Having been conditioned to accept unhappiness in childhood, they develop inhibitions which prevent them from finding day-to-day living pleasurable and enjoyable. They never realize how much *fun* they might get out of life, if they tried to change their attitudes about themselves.

Love Life: "The greatest purpose of life" (said Oliver Wendell Holmes) "is to live it." Whether your fears are real or imaginary, they will be less awesome if you strive to participate in the great happenings in the world around you. A person who seeks solitude, who wants to escape from the crowd, wishes to nurse his or her own fears and unhappiness. If you want to enjoy life, embrace the world. Interest yourself in your friends and your family. Share their joys and you will be joyful too.

People: People are more apt to accept you for what you *are* than for what you pretend to be.

Love: Love is not like snow that melts in the sun. Rather it is something that can break, but be repaired, like a fractured leg. Nevertheless, there must be a genuine desire to repair the damaged love relationship.

Since the need for affection is dominant in all of us, we can conclude that the act of loving is subconsciously motivated by our one wish or need to be loved. We demonstrate in a physical way what we would like the other person to do for us. True love, therefore, is reciprocal.

The Sex-Love Impulse: Sex can represent more than just a desire to mate. It is closely related to the impulse to love. The sex-love impulse becomes an integral part of everything we do.

The ideal sex-love relationship does not just happen, according to Dr. Caprio. It is the product of intelligent study, careful planning and above all, love on the part of both husband and wife. Your health, your marriage, your sexual fulfillment and your happiness are all dependent on the degree to which you understand what the sex-love relation is and how to attain and use it.

Enjoyment: If you want to achieve a more enjoyable way of life, you must start with yourself. You cannot expect people to change or the world to change, to suit your needs and desires. You, yourself, must change. You must make your goal a *new you*.

Self-Understanding: Self-understanding is always an asset . . . never a handicap. We suffer because we are strangers to ourselves.

Most of us go through life only half-knowing ourselves. so we use only half of our potential for confidence, for happiness, for self-enjoyment and for achievement of the goals that mean the most to us. Great areas of strength remain hidden deep within us.

Self-Improvement: If you dedicate your life to improving yourself day by day, and month by month, you will be so pleased that you will hardly notice the passage of time. You will never be bored.

Maturity: Being mature means being wise, exercising self-control, thinking things through without getting upset, and then deciding how you should act. It entails tolerance and understanding. Tolerance means a live-and-let-live philosophy of life. Understanding means being careful not to stick pins into other people's balloons.

Loneliness: Loneliness is sugar-coated self-pity. The loneliest people in the world are those who concentrate only on themselves. You will never be lonely if you show people that you care about them.

Life: If you permit others to lead your life for you, to tell you what to do, you will never have a life of your own. As Mark Twain so eloquently put it, "You will wake up one day and find you have been drunk on the smell of someone else's cork."

Mind: Your mind is the master of your life. To live right you must think right. What the mind causes, the mind can cure. We all have mind power. It can do wonders for you, if you will only make greater use of it.

THE POWER OF FAITH

To succeed and enjoy life, you need to believe in yourself. Here is what Dolly Parton, the queen of country music, had to say about herself:

> I've always had confidence and guts. I believe in positive thinking—in willing yourself to be anything you wanted to be. You know you can think yourself rich, or you can think yourself poor. You can think yourself having a horrible marriage or you can make it work. Even before I knew they wrote books on positive thinking, I grew up where *faith* was what carried us through. So I thought I want to have faith in myself. I want to be happy. I want to be a star. And I like myself. After all, it's all I got. So why can't I have the best for myself?

Our congratulations to Dolly Parton for discovering the power of faith. We hope our readers will adopt Dolly's right-to-self-happiness philosophy of life.

We all need to acquire an affirmative attitude toward life. We alone are responsible for the kind of thinking we do about ourselves and the world around us. As Dr. Norman Lunde said, "Life produces for us just what we *believe* about ourselves."

Deep down within you exists a vital living power to enjoy yourself—to live a fuller, richer life, a life you've never lived before. Faith in yourself and in a higher power can work miracles to improve your health—miracles of love, happiness and peace of mind. Seek self-enjoyment within your own heart and mind. That is the only place you'll ever find it. Remember that life is what you make it to a great extent. You weave the fabric of your destiny with your choice of life styles. The enjoyment of yourself is not dependent on riches, but on the joy and satisfaction of accomplishments that are worthwhile.

Make up your mind to be happy each and every day. And make your own happiness, for it won't come to you of its own accord.

Make the following your own special pledge of life. Carry it with you and read it over several times a day, or you may wish to memorize it. You can then say the words aloud in the morning and evening and during each day:

MY PLEDGE OF LIFE

1. I believe that happiness comes from within—a learned habit of enjoying all of the little pleasures of life as well as the major events.

2. I believe that I can enjoy one day at a time, while working toward future goals, and I will never be without an exciting goal.

3. I believe that I can survive all of life's problems and frustrations that come my way, whether I have caused them or others have caused them.

4. I believe I am capable of being happy and enjoying myself.

2
Look for Small Pleasures

Flashback. You're seated in Rick's restaurant in intriguing Casablanca. Someone at the piano begins to play a tune that sounds awfully familiar. In a few moments, a handsome man enters the main room of the restaurant and walks over quickly to the piano. "I thought I told you never to play that song, Sam!"

Yes. It's hard to forget Humphrey Bogart raising his glass toward Ingrid Bergman and saying the old familiar line: "Here's looking at you, kid!" In the scenes when he was courting her in Paris, Bogart, as Rick, flashed a smile that became part of the character he played. In effect, he was smiling at the whole silly world that was seemingly crumbling around him and the woman he loved. Nobody but Bogart could have played Rick so well. He became immortal through the role. And his cynical-looking half-smile at the crazy world around him helped him do it.

THE MAGIC OF A SMILE

One definite way to increase your own daily happiness and enjoyment of life is to focus on small pleasures. There are lots of them. Many persons miss a lot of small pleasures, simply because their field of vision only has room for four-star major ones. There are many little experiences that bring pleasure, too, that please the eye, ear, and mind, or just seem to be agreeable in their own special way.

A smile is one small pleasure. There is magic in a smile and sometimes power. The course of history, itself, has been changed by a smile. Cleopatra's smile won the hearts of Mark Antony and Julius Caesar as well. Once Elizabeth Barrett and Robbert Browning had exchanged smiles, nothing and no one (including Elizabeth's father) could keep them from eventually eloping. Think how much poorer our spinning planet would be without the value and magic of a smile.

What is this magic behind a smile? A smile lights up a person's face, makes the eyes twinkle, the lips curl a bit, and puts a crease along the cheek lines. Dr. Caprio believes that smiling can make a person feel better. A smile releases tension, relaxes the facial muscles, and makes one look far more alive.

The smiles of children remain in many minds. Remember little Shirley Temple or the smiles between Mickey Rooney and Judy Garland? One way that the Kodak Company and other camera firms sell a lot of their products these days is to show the unique smiles of children on television and in magazine ads. These color smiles create a desire in parents and relatives everywhere to capture the smiles of the children in their lives on camera.

Prisoners doing time in their cells think of the smiles of their wives or girl friends, and it helps them to get through the months and years of prison life. As the years go by, and we lose our loved ones, relatives, and friends, we remember them from the smiles they etched on our hearts, minds, and lives.

A DOZEN GREAT SMILES

1. Franklin Delano Roosevelt
2. Steve McQueen, in "The Great Escape"
3. Louis "Satchmo" Armstrong
4. Helen Hayes, First Lady of the theater
5. John F. Kennedy
6. Nancy Reagan
7. Paul Newman, in "Cool Hand Luke"
8. Jim Garner, in "Maverick"
9. Dolly Parton
10. Hubert Humphrey
11. Mary Tyler Moore
12. Gary Coleman, in "Diff'rent Strokes"

Can you add a dozen more?

Millions of people pass each other every day in all kinds of stores, shopping malls, supermarkets, and in all the market-places and halls of commerce of the world. Who knows how many of these people are worn out, discouraged, lonely, depressed, up-tight, or perhaps desperate? And then somebody passes them with a warm and pleasant smile. That smile may help them get through the day. It may well be the highlight of the week for them.

A smile is free and effortless. It reveals the inner warmth, character, friendliness, esteem, affection, or love for the person smiled at. It does so at least when it is a genuine smile.

So smile and the world will smile with you and back at you. And the shadow of your smile will be a small pleasure for others along the way.

SOME OTHER
SMALL PLEASURES OF LIFE

There are numerous other small pleasures that can and will enrich your daily life. Here are just a few of them:

1. *Fellowship with Friends.* Your visits and get-togethers with friends are small pleasures. Having lunch or dinner with a friend can lift your spirits and be a real tonic for you.

2. *The Changing Seasons.* It's easy to take the changing of the seasons for granted. It can, on the other hand, be a pleasure to watch with interest the changes that come over the land. I know, for example, that I never cease to marvel each year at the return of spring in all its glory.

3. *Interesting or Mind-Stimulating Ideas and Information.* When it comes to information and how much there is to learn about everything under the sun, mankind is much like a small child standing on the shore looking out to sea. That's how much more there is to discover and find out. The knowledge explosion continues, with no end in sight. There are ideas everywhere—bits of useful, exciting, informative, or inspiring gems of information waiting to be found.

In Atlanta recently, I visited a museum on the Emory University campus. I wanted to see the special Margaret Mitchell collection. I was so interested to see on display a copy of *Gone With the Wind*. The book was open, and I could read the lines written there by the famous author herself. Evidently, Margaret Mitchell had given this copy of her book to a friend. The date (year only) at the top was 1937. But it was the one line written by the author beneath the year that fascinated me. It read: "This is just another cheap murder story." I was astounded to learn that Margaret Mitchell thought so little of her work.

4. *Coke Floats*. The small pleasure of a coke float is a popular one with many. Summertime is a special time for cool and delightful coke floats. Some people call them black or purple cows. Others think of them as simply frosted cokes.

This drink is made by putting several dips of vanilla ice-cream into a tall glass and then filling the glass with Coca-Cola. These coke floats are marvelous and very refreshing. I enjoy them all year long at my home, but they're especially in order during the hot summer months.

During one summer a few years back, I fixed my visiting uncle from New Orleans a coke float. He had never had one before. He thought the drink was wonderful. The very next afternoon (the Fourth of July) he suddenly clapped his hands in front of everyone and announced with great gusto: "It's time for another coke float."

5. *A Morning, Afternoon, or Evening Walk*. Another of life's simple pleasures is a walk. It's amazing how taking a walk can bring enjoyment, but it does just that for millions of people everywhere.

A woman in Memphis, Tennessee walks literally every-where—to the post office, the grocery, to the building where she works, to see friends, and just about everywhere she wants to go. She claims that she's felt much happier, healthier, and more en-thused about her entire life since she started walking on a regular basis. While you may not wish (or have time) to walk this much, even a short walk each day can be beneficial to you. Scientists have found that walking and jogging relieve depression.

There's little doubt that walking is an enjoyable experi-ence for a great many persons. You can enjoy the scenery while walking, think out a question or problem, or just enjoy the walk itself. The great short story writer Edgar Allen Poe worked on stories and other creative projects in his mind while walking.

On the celebration of his ninety-second birthday, William Wright, one of the last soldier veterans of the Boer War, was asked for his secret for a long life. Wright's answer was "a six-mile hike every day with a rest stop at the local pub for a visit with good friends."

So making better use of your two feet is a pleasure. Walk for fun. Walk for health. Walk for enjoyment and adventure. Walk to see more of the world around you. Walk for new ideas. You'll be glad you did.

6. Humming a Favorite Song or Tune. Nostalgia has been quite the rage in recent years. And one of the direct ways in which the memories of the past come rolling back is via the great old songs and tunes of yesterday.

Just today, after lunch, I found myself humming a popular tune called "Lady of Spain." I kept humming the familiar melody, without knowing the title of the song at first. I really enjoyed hearing the tune again and felt better all day for it.

Breaking into a hum of your favorite tunes can be a daily pleasure and quick source of enjoyment. It can do you good to hear some of the wonderful songs of recent years or even those of long past eras. "It Had to Be you," "Tea for Two," "Cruising Down the River," "Linda," "It's a Good Day," "Yesterday," and "April Showers" are just a few of the tunes that continually pop into my mind, demanding to be given the center stage spotlight again.

In your mind, you can hear again at will the memorable songs from the last several years and those from way back too. Such tunes have taken on a life of their own in a great many memories. But it's even more fun and enjoyable to hum them as you go along your way.

You can think of many other simple pleasures to add to those in this chapter. If you agree that the following additional items belong on your own personal list of small pleasures, place a check mark in the space to the right of each item. And feel free to make any additions to this list as shown below:

7. A Cold (or Warm) Glass of Milk Before Bedtime

_____

8. Watching a Dawn or Sunset _____

9. Greeting a Dog, Cat, or Other Pet, After You've Been Away Some Time _____

10. A Hot Cup of Coffee, Tea, or Cocoa on a Cold Day _____

11. Admiring Your Car After You've Washed It Yourself _____

12. Seeing a Good Movie on the Late Show _____

13. The Fresh Air of a Delightful Summer Breeze _____

14. The Strange and Silent Beauty of Snow, as it Blankets the Land _____

15. The Laughter of Children (or Someone You Love) _____

16. The Sight of the Flag Going by in a Parade _____

17. Lying on a Beach and Listening to the Relentless Sound of the Surf _____

18. The Smell of Fresh-Baked Bread or Cookies _____

19. Singing "Happy Birthday" to a Friend or Loved One _____

20. Gazing at the Endless Number of Stars on a Clear and Beautiful Night _____

21. The Sight of Friendly Leaves Drifting by Your Window on a Crisp Fall Day _____

22. The Thrill of a Long and Beautiful Pass, Completed by Your Favorite Football Team _____

23. Roasting Hot Dogs on a Campfire _____

24. Holding Hands With the One You Love _____

25. Browsing in a Good Bookstore _____

There you have them. The above list is by no means a complete one. But the twenty-five items named give a good idea of some of the many small pleasures life offers you. Try not to miss these little pleasures in life, for they are all around you each day. Look for them and enjoy them, too, along with the four-star pleasures.

The small pleasures of life are like a string of pearls laid out over many years. Be alert for them. Appreciate them. Experience and enjoy them to the fullest. For they, too, do much to make your life sweet and dear.

3
Take the Strain
Out of Decision-Making

When it's time to make decisions, a great many people feel the desire to run. A period of strain and confusion sets in, and it can be a difficult period for many persons. Certainly there are times when the decisions being made are crucial ones. The best bet is to head off these important decision-making moments by being more prepared for them in advance.

You've heard many times that the art of decision-making takes courage. It does. Some people admit to their close friends that they find decision-making a hard thing to do. There are reasons why people get bogged down with many decisions. One of these reasons is the pressure of a deadline. Many decisions need to be made within a certain time or by a specific date. As the deadline gets nearer, with no real decision made, the pressure naturally increases. It's much like delaying the completion of your income tax until very close to the last day.

The time taken to make decisions is more important than most of us realize.

ALL KINDS OF DECISIONS TO MAKE

Ever think about how many different decisions you make? Career decisions? How about family decisions? What to wear to work tomorrow, what to order for lunch, should you go ahead with an investment you've both been thinking about, should the kids have a larger allowance, should you keep the car another year or trade it in?

The swine flu snafu during President Gerald Ford's last year in office will no doubt be talked and written about for a long time to come. Many are still firmly convinced that it was political. Any way you look at it, the entire plan for flu shots for the nation was badly managed and perhaps unnecessary . . . judging by only a small number of flu cases that later developed. For millions of people, it meant still another decision—to get the shot or not.

A President's Tough Decision

President Ford had some tough decisions to make during his stay in the White House. Many of those who voted for or against Ford believe that the pardon of Richard Nixon was what prevented Ford from being elected to a full four-year term of his own. But look at it from Ford's viewpoint. Ford must have known that such a decision would surely cost him and hurt his chances to stay in the White House.

Still asked today about his key decision to pardon Nixon, Ford continues to defend his decision as a sound one: "I issued the pardon, because in the first month that I was president, we had horrendous problems in Southeast Asia and Vietnam. And all the time in that first month there was controversy day after day. I was spending at least 25 percent of my time listening to legal arguments about what we would do with the Nixon papers . . . at a time when I should have been working 100 percent of the time on the war in Vietnam and the problems of the economy and that is the only reason that I really made the decision."

The art and/or science of making wise decisions used to be thought of as mainly a man's arena. Not any more. Women today are making just as crucial decisions as men both on and off the job. Millions of American women are juggling both paid employment and homemaking chores and decisions. A survey conducted by Market Opinion Research revealed that nine out of ten women have worked for payment at sometime in their lives. About 42 percent are in the labor force today, but this figure may continue to rise.

FOUR KEY STEPS FOR BETTER DECISION-MAKING

Granted that the ability to make decisions is vital—no matter what one's position is—what can help you to develop more courage for facing crucial decisions? Four key questions suggested by Dr. Caprio, can be a real aid to you for all those decisions you'll be making in the months and years ahead. You can profit by keeping these four questions in mind.

1. What Do You Need to Decide?

In other words, what information, knowledge, or material do you need to have on hand before trying to arrive at a decision? Whatever it may be, try to obtain the needed information. It will usually speed up your decision. Having all the facts is quite important, because it takes the guesswork out of decision-making. You can be sure that every president who has arrived at any number of decisions in the famed oval office has had plenty of facts for company.

2. What Must Be Decided?

A second key question that can inspire more courage for your crucial decisions is this one: What must you decide? Be very clear about what it is. Write it down. Express or sum it up simply and directly as possible. Believe it or not, many decision makers are often confused as to just what has to be decided. State the problem or thing to be decided and make sure that you understand it completely.

3. Is There Anything Else You Must Know?

For a third aid in reaching a decision, ask yourself if there's anything else that you need to know. You might be leaving out one or more facts or vital bits of information necessary to arrive at a right solution. Have you forgotten anything? Have you considered the problem from all sides and examined all points or aspects of it? Every time the great inventor Thomas Edison failed to find something that would work for his invention of the electric light, he just figured that he was a little bit closer to the right answer. With each failure (and he had quite a few of them), he moved on to another attempt, wondering what else to try. What else? That was his continual question.

4. What Are Your Alternatives?

A fourth question to ask yourself is how can you make a particular decision? What are your alternatives, when it comes to the decision itself? What other avenues does your decision open up and involve? There may be some clues here that can help you to reach a better decision.

When the cry of gold echoed across the nation in the late 1840s, a brave and vigorous group could not resist the call. Their alternative to striking out for the West and a chance to find gold, not to mention the adventure and challenge of building a new life, was to stay home and continue their routine lives. The alternative was too weak to compare with the excitement of joining the crowds heading west. The lure of gold in the West was too strong.

Think of what a decision it was for them to give up their homes and farmlands to move westward, in wagons filled with their families and belongings. With the ring of adventure in their hearts and the dream of riches in their blood, they made their decision and pointed their teams west.

Some crucial decisions can cost a lot. In the case of the forty-niners, it was a big price. It was paid in grueling overland travel, dust and sand storms, disease, starvation on the long (often three- to four-month) journey, and the constant threat of Indian attack.

But look at the fruitful results of their decision. Despite all their hardships and difficulties, some 50,000 forty-niners were lured to California in 1849. The streets of San Francisco swarmed with newcomers, and many of them spoke foreign languages, as new arrivals from other countries.

The spirit, courage, and daring of their decision to settle in the West paid off in different ways. Most of them never found gold, but their lives were still enriched in other ways. *They found a new beginning*—a fresh start in a new land. New opportunities were realized by many, because they were there in the early history of California. Many who stayed in California played their own parts in building that state.

The forty-niners have a unique place in our history. Their determination and decisive action, in the face of great odds, has helped to keep alive the true spirit of the American tradition. In their fight to win a fortune, they helped build a mighty land.

Nobody Bats a Perfect Decision Record

Everyone must make decisions from the early childhood days to the grave. The better we can get at doing it, the more confidence we'll have in ourselves and our own judgment. Do your best, but recognize also that nobody bats a perfect record at making crucial decisions or even the regular, easier ones. Get all the facts you possibly can, ask yourself these related questions, and you will usually be able to reach a fairly sound decision. Sometimes sleeping on it will help you decide. But usually only a period of time and experience will tell if you've made the right decision or not. If you haven't, then resolve to do better on the next ones coming your way.

4

How to Get More Humor in Your Life

"Have you heard about my million dollar movie offer? If I pay a million dollars, they'll let me be in the movie."

Credit for this joke goes to John Coleman, the genial weatherman of television's number one news and information program—"Good Morning, America." Coleman has a marvelous sense of humor. Granted that his joke (which he cracked recently) may not be of vintage quality, it's impossible to watch and hear Coleman give the weather each day without often being amused by his remarks.

Coleman is a real pro weatherman, mind you, but the way he adds little touches of humor add much to the weather side of the morning program. He is most certainly a very entertaining weatherman. He makes the weather report interesting. John Coleman actually makes you look forward to seeing the weather news. You never know what he's going to say next.

Dr. Caprio has long believed that a sense of humor throughout life is as essential to normal living as oxygen is to the lungs. Laughter is an antidote for the day-to-day frustrations that can destroy a healthy person as inexorably as some great tragedy. A sense of humor lifts the emotional strain in which you may hold yourself. It thrusts aside your gloomy thoughts. Humor helps you to relax. It pulls up those saggy facial muscles and sad-dened eyes to a refreshing smile. It takes you away from your perhaps often dull routine, your disturbing thoughts. Humor brings a change you must have. The counterbalance it provides is essential in an age of work and worry.

After forty years of giving talks or lectures to a variety of audiences (including television and radio appearances), I have discovered that almost everyone appreciates humor as evidenced by a smile, a chuckle or outright laughter. An audience likes to learn, but it also likes to be entertained. At least that has been my experience. I have made it a point to incorporate into every lecture something that will make people laugh—a humorous anecdote—or a joke I felt was right for the subject of my talk. Let me cite an example of how I began a particular lecture: "The other day I had my regular checkup from my doctor, a cardiologist who had been treating me. When he finished his examination he said: 'At your age you should give up half of your sex life, to avoid undue excitement.' I replied: 'Which half, doctor, do you want me to give up? The half I think about or the half I talk about?'"

YOU *CAN* DEVELOP A STRONGER SENSE OF HUMOR

Can anyone develop a sense of humor? Of course. There are numerous paperbacks that are devoted to jokes. You can memorize a dozen or more of them that are favorites for you and practice telling them to small social groups. Determine to tell at least one or two jokes every opportunity you have to a receptive audience. You should make sure, however, that the jokes you relate are not in bad taste or offensive. And avoid ethnic jokes that may offend some of the people you may not know too well and who may be sensitive. Their reaction will be definitely unfavorable. Don't worry about a joke being old. A good joke is ageless and there are always those who haven't heard it.

It takes practice to become a good storyteller at parties, or in your talks or lectures. You have to become a collector of jokes, both new ones and those you have heard from friends. You can write them down or keep them in a file box. You can also use the technique of describing some of the funny cartoons you encounter in magazines. In addition, you can memorize a number of humorous one-liners like "Sex is here to stray."

The person who has mastered the art of making people laugh finds life more enjoyable. Bob Hope gets a great deal of personal satisfaction out of bringing enjoyment to the millions of his fans. But you don't have to be a professional comedian to cultivate a sense of humor. It's a learning technique, like learning to dance or drive a car.

To steal someone else's jokes is not a crime. The next time you tune in on a comedian, have your pencil and notebook ready. Jot down the best jokes and then memorize them. Pass them on. It's a way of adding to your popularity. Try it. Laughter has healing powers. It's an antidepressant and a tranquilizer.

Humor Relieves Boredom

One of the best things about humor is that it often dissipates boredom. Humor is also a relief from guilt or depressed feelings, tension, headaches and backaches.

Some say that boredom is the absence of happiness.

Shocking as it may seem, cultivating a stronger and sharper sense of humor can even save lives. Boredom, often a reflection of a deeper depression problem, actually killed film actor George Sanders. When he took his own life in Spain some years ago, he left a note behind saying: "I've lived too long, and I'm bored."

Why are so many people bored today? A basic reason for this widespread boredom is because—more than ever before—a great many people in today's world have been everywhere, seen everything, and "done it all," as some of them put it. Children, for example, don't have time to be children anymore. They have to grow up too fast. They are forced by television and the fast pace of today's modern life to "know it all" by the time they reach the teenage years. So it's little wonder that they're bored in their twenties or thirties. In a real sense, they're old-timers by then.

Laughter Does Wonders for You

You may be surprised to hear that laughter is healthy for you. It is quite true. Studies show that laughter stimulates the human brain to produce hormones called catecholamines. These hormones decrease arthritis pain and alleviate serious allergy problems. Here are some more specific benefits of this wonder-worker called laughter:

- When you laugh, your heart, thorax, abdomen, diaphragm, and lungs are exercised.
- Laughter helps your entire respiratory system (by cleaning it out).
- Laughter increases your heart rate and overall circulation.
- Uproarious laughter (the really crack-your-ribs kind) gives the muscles in your arms, legs, and face a workout.
- Laughter helps keep you well . . . and for longer periods of time.

In the words of Dr. William Fry, of Stanford University Medical School's psychiatry department, "Humor stirs the inside and gets the endocrine system going, which can be quite beneficial in alleviating disease."

Getting More Humor in Your Life

Don't tell yourself that humor, or the lack of it, is automatic at birth. There's a lot you can do to get more laughter into your life. Here are some proven steps for developing a keener sense of humor:

1. Think about humor more . . . and what is funny or amusing.

2. Stay alert to the sources of humor all around you (in newspapers, books, magazines, newsletters, on radio-television, cartoons, comic strips, greeting cards, and just about everywhere that human beings live and work.

3. Understand what humor actually is: "A comic quality causing amusement: the humor of a situation." It has also been defined as "the faculty of perceiving what is amusing or comical."

4. Experiment in taking something known and familiar and then making it seem funny. To do this, use the tools of association, understatement, and plain surprise. Exaggeration may also be used. Many jokes are built around some exaggeration. Satire, sarcasm, plays on words, parody and burlesque are all sources of humor and offer tips for making something funny.

5. Keep an ongoing humor book in which you write down the funny ideas and humorous bits you discover and come

across. This is an excellent way to train your mind to spot humor.

6. You can even make a game out of looking for humor. Challenge a friend, family member, or neighbor to see which one of you can come up with the best new bit of humor in the space of a weekend, a week, or longer.

Be especially alert for humorous signs. There are lots of them out there wherever you live or travel. But you have to watch for them. Here are just a few of the many amusing signs that have caught my own eye:

- "Be careful driving. Clarksville is full of Oldsmobiles and Cadillacs." (a sign seen at the city limits)
- "No shirts, no shoes, no service (a sign in a Louisville, Kentucky restaurant)
- "You don't have to be a stripper to drop your clothes here." (a sign in a Los Angeles cleaners)
- "Fight pollution. Ride a horse." (a sign on back of a car)

Remember. The trouble with most of us is that we're about 100 laughs behind. "Laugh and the world laughs with you" may be an old cliché, but it's really good advice. Learn to laugh at yourself first and then at the many funny things about life and the world, and you're bound to be a happier person. There is humor all around you everyday, if you will learn to spot it, collect it, appreciate it, and share it with others.

Laughter and humor are part and parcel of what makes life worth living. Humor is a magic elixir that will enrich your life in many ways. Start enjoying more of it at once. To laugh a lot is to have lived a fuller and more enjoyable life.

5

Enjoyable Living
Is a Science and an Art

While visiting in America a few years ago, British psychiatrist Joan Gomez was so shocked by the looks, health, and mortality rate of American men that she wrote a book about it called *How Not to Die Young*.

Dr.Gomez, who holds three degrees, feels that American men (and Americans in general) ought to be among the longest-lived peoples in the world. The medical discoveries are unique in America, and the nation's health facilities are the finest.

Perhaps the fast pace of life today is having an effect on both American men and women. Dr. Caprio believes the modern tempo of restless living has speeded up our metabolism and has thus altered our habits of eating and sleeping, to the extent that few of us know how to live properly.

BETTER LIVING HABITS BRING A MORE ENJOYABLE LIFE

There is no general formula regarding living habits merely because they vary with types of individuals as hats differ in size and style. He or she dresses well who wears that which flatters him, and similarly that person lives well whose habits best fit his or her needs.

All of us have food idiosyncrasies, and we all differ in our requirements for sleep and rest. A good case can be made for living in moderation by avoiding excesses. Resolve to eat less and to get enough sleep. Osler, the famous physician, advised every person after fifty to modify his diet; to eat less and to abate every seven years until he leaves life as he entered it on the diet of a child.

In regard to sleep, it is essential to life and necessary to restore energy, by relieving fatigue. The average person requires about eight hours of sleep. But here, again, the need of individuals may vary widely. Thomas Edison long boasted that he could thrive on four hours of sleep, but in later years he increased this amount somewhat. This is one of the things which each person must work out for himself. The purpose of sleep is for rest and refreshment. Take what you need, be it more or less than the average.

What about diet and common sense? The simple truth is that diet is decidedly a personal matter. If there is a single ideal diet well-adapted to all of us, science has yet to discover it. Each individual case requires study and experiment. A considerable number of factors must be taken into account. It is not well to be too dogmatic in laying down rules and regulations. Diets have changed materially from generation to generation, and even today the peoples of the world continue to thrive on an astonishing variety of foodstuffs.

Food fads are based on human ignorance and gullibility. Americans in particular are pathetically eager to believe everything they are told—even inaccurately reported theories that find their way into print concerning food and the mysterious miracles it can perform upon the human system.

Yes, there are some peculiar notions about food. And like a majority of mass-circulated ideas, many of them have little or no foundation in fact.

Your diet should be a sound, sane diet, carefully calculated to meet your needs of the moment and to accomplish the beneficial results that are desired and supervised by your physician.

SELF-IMPROVEMENT IS THE KEY TO SELF-ENJOYMENT

You are urged to copy the twenty-five points enumerated below and to keep the list with you. Make each one a self-improvement goal. It will take effort and a do-it-yourself determination, but you can do it.

1. Improve your sense of values
2. Achieve healthier and happier living
3. Survive adversities
4. Develop poise and tranquility
5. Change your pattern of thinking for the better
6. Live a well-balanced life
7. Master your fears
8. Acquire a better understanding of yourself
9. Live a longer and more abundant life
10. Build self-confidence
11. Get your problems into focus
12. Learn to make sound decisions
13. Improve your personality
14. Become easier to get along with
15. Develop a sense of humor
16. Believe in yourself
17. Influence your future
18. Attain your goals in life
19. Do things in moderation
20. Practice self-discipline
21. Find happiness
22. Make your mind work for you
23. Forget the past and profit from your mistakes
24. Give, accept and share love
25. Adopt a philosophy or way of life that will bring you peace of mind; that will give meaning to your life

Self-improvement will enable you to develop a healthier philosophy of life. You will be better prepared to enjoy the days, weeks, months, and years ahead of you. Despite the many people who are unhappy (and therefore aren't enjoying life), there are just as many who are glad to be alive, who appreciate all the things that are beautiful in the world.

People who confess to being happy and admit they are enjoying life have many things in common. They have the ability to assume responsibility without too many complaints, to be self-sustaining, to accept reality, and to get along with others. They have a flexible personality and can adapt themselves to many changing situations. They possess self-confidence. They are able to keep their emotions under the control of their intellect. They are tactful, have a sense of humor, are tolerant, unselfish and not oversensitive. They take criticism well and are cheerful in their dispositions. They make every attempt not to give in to anger, jealousy, or hatred. They have the capacity to love and make life pleasant for themselves instead of painful. Their happiness comes from within. They have become the kind of persons they prefer to be. They find enjoyment in their accomplishments.

MAKE EACH NEW DAY AN ENJOYABLE DAY

Each morning when you awake, resolve to make *a new begin-ning*. Make each day a good day . . . add life to your years and not merely years to your life.

Every day should bring a new passion for living—a new day to enjoy the fruits of life that you so richly deserve—a new day to learn and accomplish what you set out to do. You can gen-erate a determined resolution to live today, tomorrow and every new day with a positive attitude toward yourself and life. Start with the premise that life *can* be beautiful . . . that life is to be en-joyed. The real enjoyment of life begins with inner contentment and self-happiness.

A young patient whom I shall refer to as Kathy related how she was never able to enjoy life . . . only because she wasn't as pretty as her sister. Her mother unfortunately reminded her how different she looked and pointed out to relatives and friends how much she looked like her father (a particularly unattractive person).

Kathy became extremely self-conscious and experienced states of chronic depression. She felt she was doomed because of her inferiority complex and would never find enjoyment in life. She finally realized that she was indulging in negative over-compensation (self-pity) for her inferiority feelings. She learned to like herself, to love life, to improve her personality, and most important of all that she was entitled to enjoy herself . . . that life was meant to be enjoyed.

Two Questions to Ask Yourself

R. William Whitmer, executive director of Wellness Centers of America, says there are two basic questions people rarely ask themselves. Whitmer thinks both should be asked:

1. How long will I live?
2. Am I really feeling as good as I possibly can?

Whitmer firmly believes that the way you treat your body has a definite effect on how good you feel and how long you'll be around. Whitmer conducts wellness seminars around the country and discusses six negative lifestyles: lack of regular exercise, too much alcohol, and smoking, obesity, poor nutrition and a poor handling of stress.

As Whitmer puts it, "We try to get people to realize that the negative lifestyle they are leading does destroy vital organs and life systems. People in this day and age have become so sophisticated because of the various media, it's not like it was thirty or fifty years ago. People are finally realizing, 'I can understand some of this stuff.' "

Always keep in mind that exercise is a real aid to mental relaxation. Along with strengthening your muscles, exercise also frees the mind of its cares.

It should be obvious that a laborer in a steel mill and the president of a bank need *different* types of diversional activities. The laborer might find relaxation in reading the current installment of a spellbinding detective story, while the bank president prefers to relieve his accumulated nervous tension by pulling weeds out of his garden. A salesman leading a busy pavement-pounding daily routine might find greater enjoyment in some confining activity such as stamp collecting, instead of seeking to build up his already weary muscles through monotonous body-building exercises.

In matching your physical and mental requirements with your occupation or vocation, select the activity that seems to best satisfy your individual needs.

In Washington, D.C., many of the congressmen and senators have the right idea in barring all mention of politics during the course of games or exercise. The program offers a rather elaborate system for the soothing of nerves and the relaxation of tired muscles. The system consists of a long tub soak, a salt rub and an electrical dry-out, followed by muscle massage.

As you probably have gathered, the whole idea is to get some *fun* out of whatever you do for relaxation. Unless you enjoy your exercise, it's the wrong kind of exercise for you and is probably doing you more harm than good. Stop it and take up something that interests you—something, if possible, that will combine brain relaxation with muscle stimulation.

Film actress Katharine Hepburn enjoys exercise. She thrives on physical and mental activity. "Exercise, which I love, keeps me in shape. And I do get sufficient rest. As heavy as I eat, that's how heavy I sleep. Whether I'm eating, sleeping, or working, I enjoy myself."

Once you develop a stronger sense of inner happiness and enjoyment of life, you will find that it has an influence on your way of thinking and your overall philosophy of living. As an example, here is one man's view or attitude on self-enjoyment, as expressed by Frank Capri, a journalist-photographer in Hollywood, California: "Out of a strong sense of inner happiness and enjoyment of life, I hope to touch the world. I'm happy to say, in general (when I'm not lapsing into negative thinking), that I love myself and human beings everywhere. Certainly I have differences with many people, but I accept the fact that we are all one family. America is a family. Humankind is a family."

Enjoyable living is healthy, stimulating, and cleansing. It is well worth the effort. Heed this advice from Florence Nightingale: "Live your life while you have it. Life is a splendid gift. There is nothing small in it. For the greatest things grow by God's law out of the smallest. But to live your life (and enjoy it) well takes discipline."

Whenever you may find yourself drifting from the road of enjoyable living, turn back to this chapter and apply the steps discussed. You will then be able to climb back on the right road. For the most part, enjoyable living is what you make it.

6

"O" Is for Organization

If there's one single password to more enjoyment and effectiveness in your work, that key word is organization. As a better organized person, you'll save time, accomplish more during your on-the-job hours, and feel more confident about your work.

The truth is that a single day can make a difference, if you're well organized There are only twenty-four hours in a day. If you don't plan your time well, it's simply going to slip by. The approximate eight hours you spend at work five days a week (not counting the time you have off for lunch) can be far more productive ones when and if you are organized.

HOW TO BECOME BETTER ORGANIZED

Dr. Caprio believes that many workers have nothing to do for part of their work day. Some of each work day is thus wasted due to poor organization.

Here are some proven guidelines for being a better organized person. These suggestions apply regardless of whether you're an average worker or an executive:

1. If you believe you're in the wrong kind of work (for you), and still see yourself as unhappy in the same job years from now, start making plans now to get into work you will like or be better suited for.

Bob Mills found out that practicing law in San Francisco was not for him. He knew at the same time that he had always liked writing. He began sending one-line jokes to a local disc jockey. The happy result was that Mills was encouraged to continue writing. He moved to Hollywood and wrote for some television shows. Mills is a top joke writer today for comedian Bob Hope.

2. Be certain that you have a clear understanding of what is expected of you in your job. This is especially important in the early weeks and months of a position.

3. See if the duties of your position offer a curiosity potential. In other words, determine if there's some aspect of your work that arouses your curiosity or additional interest. Many successful workers and employees make a practice of staying curious about new approaches to their work. How can some parts of your work be performed more efficiently? What new ideas or changes might upgrade the productivity of your work (or your department, group, plant, or office)?

The answers to the following questions can help you to become a more organized and efficient worker:

- How can I do my job better?
- How can I save my boss or employer more time?
- Do I have any ideas for other departments or branches of my company?
- Is there some area of my work I could study more or investigate?
- Would my arriving at the office an hour earlier (or staying an hour later) help me become better organized?

Consider this idea. If you learned just one new and useful fact about your job or work each day for the next 365 days, you would be well on your way to becoming an expert.

4. Lie in bed for fifteen or twenty minutes each work day morning. In your mind, go over the day ahead of you and decide how you might better perform your work. This has been a helpful method for many people everywhere.

5. Keep an ongoing diary or work record. Write down

any and all ideas you get for saving time and being better organized. Pool such ideas and suggestions from all sources (books,
magazines, bulletins, business reports, conferences, meetings at
the office, and your own imagination).

6. Write yourself little notes, hints, or tips that will help you
do better work. Place these notes where you will see them daily at
your office, desk, a bulletin board, at home, or wherever. A variation of this is to carry three-by-five inch note cards in your pocket or
purse. This will assure that you see and read them each day.

7. Promote the idea of regular brainstorming sessions to
be held for those in your group, office, plant, company, department, or branch. Such sessions act on the rule that several or
more heads are better than one. During these meetings, brain-
storm for:

☐ better organization in general
☐ better solutions to stubborn problems
☐ better plans for a smoother-running office or operation

8. Don't count on the officers or managers of your company to provide you with all the answers. Seek the answers yourself and then pass them along—especially your ideas for better
work flow and overall improvement.

9. Sometimes careful study on the negative aspects of
your work can help you to spot solutions. Some specific examples might be too much paperwork, messy files, no inter-
change of ideas, the lack of quality communication among
departments or groups, and poorly defined work goals.

10. Check frequently to see if the following specific acts
of organization may be necessary in your work:

☐ Clean off your desk.
☐ Start a new and better filing system.
☐ Write important memos to yourself on goals.
☐ Make lists to jog your memory.
☐ Get unpleasant tasks done and out of the way.
☐ Return all phone calls at once or as soon as possible.

11. Try to appreciate the work you do. It's the working men and women who have kept this country and world moving forward. They put food on the table during the depression years. The working people built the planes, tanks, and jeeps (plus all the rest of the equipment necessary) for victory during war. Working people pay the taxes that run the nation, support the congress, and maintain a strong national defense. Be proud to be a member of the work force.

When and where you see the need for improvements, solutions, or an upgrading of quality, do what you can to upgrade the system. What you do may have a strong and continuing influence.

When asked by a fellow worker why he was quitting a job (and a good one at that), a computer employee replied that "lawyers and accountants steal from their clients, government agencies cheat each other, suppliers steal from the companies they serve, foremen steal from each other, and we, the computer industry, computerize it all for them."

Make this your daily motto and repeat it to yourself aloud each morning, before leaving for work: "Today I will do my level best in my job (work, position, or profession). I will strive to stay organized as best I can and to perform my work as efficiently and productively as possible." Do that, and you'll find that you'll get more enjoyment out of your work, as well as a more enjoyable day.

7

The Best Way to Handle
Blue Mondays

One of the most popular radio programs, when radio offered more than music, sports, and news, was an exciting weekly drama called "Escape." The program always began with the announcer's voice asking, "Tired of the weekend? Does blue Monday stare you in the face? We offer you escape."

The invitation to escape, by listening to the program, was hard to resist. Millions acted on the invitation each week. As each new Monday rolls around in real life, many people shrink from the necessity of returning to the job and daily routine. Blue Mondays are tough to handle for millions.

A grind. That's what many members of the work force call the work week schedules they put in week after week. Blue Mondays often make workers wonder how on earth they'll be able to pull themselves back to work on Monday. It's just tough for many to return, much less keep at it until Friday. You may well have experienced the same feeling yourself.

What's happened to these unhappy people? Why are their jobs apparently seen as slave labor? It's not just the poor job or low income workers who are affected by the start of a new work week. Many with interesting and well-paid positions have to drive themselves back on Monday morning. Perhaps everyone sooner or later is caught up in the blue Monday doldrums, but there's no need for it. Such low spirits, or the blues, or feelings of depression, can be fought and overcome. Blue Mondays can be met head on and conquered. By changing your attitude and thinking, and resisting negative thoughts, you can even turn your blue Mondays into the most valuable day of the week.

The first thing to do in this new way of thinking for happier work weeks is to see each Monday as a fresh start offering new opportunities and potential. Many successful salespeople are actually eager to get to work on Mondays, because they know if they can make some good sales that first day the momentum of that positive encouragement will carry them through a successful week of many sales.

No Two Mondays Are Alike

Whatever your work may be, no two Mondays are going to be exactly alike. There is bound to be at least some variety from one to another. You probably don't eat lunch at the same place every day. Try to see the new opportunities of each Monday. Try to do all you can in your present work, and one day you may find that you've grown larger than your present position. New work more to your liking may then open up for you.

A Proven Way to Fight Blue Mondays

One proven way to fight blue Mondays with success is to decide in your mind before Monday ever dawns that it's going to be a happy and successful day. See yourself going to work with a positive frame of mind and performing your work with skill and enthusiasm all day long. Try this for six straight Mondays and see what happens. You may be surprised.

Don't let negative thoughts ambush your good Monday intentions either. They'll be trying to take over your thinking. You can also use this same method for any other day of the week—days that are generally dismal for you. Monday is the worst for most people.

Use the Role Playing Idea

Another thought to consider each weekend, before Monday stares you in the face, is a role-playing idea. Imagine what you would do if you had no job at all . . . no work to go to on Mondays. Unless you have an independent source of money that keeps coming in, you're like the large majority of people; you must work at something that pays your bills and supports you as well as possible.

Such thinking will make you appreciate your work like never before, for you're seeing it in a new light. Think of the millions now out of work in the country. Whatever your work is, it does support you and provide you with gainful employment until more interesting work presents itself. Nothing says you are in your present work for life. In your free time, find what you want to do, study it, plan for the day you can make the change. In a truer sense than anyone realizes, each one of us is the captain of his or her own destiny.

Some Causes of Blue Mondays

One basic cause of so-called blue Mondays is simply physical weariness. Lots of workers try to do too much in one short weekend. Staying up to all hours all weekend, then driving yourself too much during Saturday and Sunday, is bound to be reflected in one tired human being on Monday morning. Many feel they must jump in their cars and drive a hundred or so miles each way—just for a few hours at some resort—and yet such a determined effort to earn some rest and relaxation can be self-defeating. Weekend trips are fine if they are short ones, giving you enough time to get back home without having to drive like the Dukes of Hazzard. An effective and productive week of work does take its toll, so give your body a break by resting at least a little on the weekends. You don't have to lie around all weekend, but you need some "hammock time" before Monday rolls around.

Workaholics and Moonlighters

While there are those who play too much, there are also many others who don't seem to know how to turn off the work juice. America, more than any other country, has become a moonlighting nation. The number of workers holding down two and even three jobs in America is astounding, and it's constantly growing. Leading doctors, Dr. Caprio for one, cite such continuous work without a letup as a prime cause of heart attacks. The traditional proverb, "All work and no play makes Jack a dull boy" is true. The same goes for all play and no work. Try to balance your life with enough work, but know how to relax as well. A proper balance of the two is what sustains vitality.

Another big reason why millions find themselves uptight on Monday mornings is the utter loneliness of their weekends. Trapped in big cities, they feel miserable all weekend, usually spending their time alone. To buck up their low spirits, they may turn to alcohol or drugs. When Monday morning finally rolls around, they can hardly roll out of bed. Who would feel like starting a new week with a hangover? Many do just that. Others are caught like social rats on the party circuit, boozing it up until their money runs out or they're out cold. Is it any wonder they don't feel like returning to work on Monday?

The abuse of television viewing may well leave many persons with a drugged or depressed feeling. The wonders of television are captivating, but too much of it is a time killer.

Keep your body in good condition so it can do its best for your future. Take care of it so it can take care of you.

Keep in Mind the Good Things About Work

Perhaps the soundest way to handle any and all blue Mondays, or any day of the week for that matter, is to admit and realize the many good things about work itself. Thomas Carlyle, the Scottish writer, said it well: "Blessed is he who has found his work; let him ask no other blessedness. He has a work, a life-purpose; he has found it, and will follow it." If you haven't found your real work yet, get busy and start looking for it. Seek clues. There's a right place and work for you. What is it that you can do better than most others? If it is something that you enjoy and it offers you a productive, honest income (with the chance to grow), get into it. Start part-time if you must, until you can move into it on a full-time basis.

Once in the right place for you . . . and there *is* a right work for you . . . you'll find yourself eager for Monday mornings. An interest and liking for what you're doing is the key to a happier and certainly a more productive work life. After all, a major part of your life is spent working. So it might as well be work you are interested in doing. To really achieve and accomplish something in your work, you're going to have to like it. You can't imagine how much happier you'll be when you have found the type of work that is right for you. There are enough round pegs in square holes today. Seek your true work with all your heart.

Some People Live for Their Work

"My destiny is solitude, and my life is work," said Richard Wagner, the great German composer. It is true that in all ages people have lived for their work. Some never find love, a home and family of their own, so the great joy of their lives must come in their work.

Love your work, and you will not be denied that priceless sense of satisfaction found in a life well spent. Who knows? Through you and the work you perform, it is quite possible that the world can become a better place . . . a happier planet. Small or great, you can make a worthwhile contribution through your productive work years. Above all, you'll be at peace with yourself in suitable work which holds your interest; work that perhaps challenges you and calls for your finest effort.

Henry Ward Beecher once said: "When God wanted sponges and oysters, He made them, and put one on a rock, and the other in the mud. When He made man, He did not make him to be a sponge, or an oyster; He made him with feet, and hands, and head, and heart, and vital blood, and a place to use them, and said to him, "Go, work."

8

Avoiding and Overcoming
Job Burnout

A burned-out human being is a sad figure to behold. The person is existing, but that's about all. The interest in life, the challenge of each new day, the enthusiasm, zip and spark of personality are gone. Life has become a series of wooden, hollow actions for a victim of burnout. You just could care less. There's little or no meaning anymore. Many people who are suffering from burnout are walking "zombies."

The following short test is meant to help you determine how near or far from burnout you may be at present. Answer each question with a "yes" or "no." Then add up your total score:

	Yes	No
1. Do you feel tired and run-down a great deal of the time?	_____	_____
2. Do you seem to be cross and irritable a lot . . . and for no apparent reason?	_____	_____
3. Do you have too many drinks in the course of a day or week?	_____	_____
4. Do you find that you can't seem to get things done anymore, although you spend a lot of time at work?	_____	_____
5. Do you often (or usually) work a twelve-hour day (or longer)?	_____	_____
6. Do you sometimes skip an annual vacation and spend holidays doing additional work?	_____	_____

	Yes	No
7. Do you frequently feel helpless?	_____	_____
8. Do you feel like you've been in a pressure cooker at the end of the day or week?	_____	_____
9. Do you take work home with you several nights a week or over the weekend?	_____	_____
10. Do you feel that you continually have to prove yourself?	_____	_____

Score ten points for each "yes" answer and add up your total. Here is an evaluation of your score:

_____ a score of 100   — You are now a victim of burnout.

_____ a score of 90   — You are close to "burning out."

_____ a score of 80   — There are signs of potential burnout in your life.

A BASIC CAUSE OF BURNOUT

One of the major reasons for burnout says Dr. Caprio, is overextending yourself. You expect too much of yourself. Here are some examples:

• An executive may overextend himself or herself by refusing to quit working. Many executives feel guilty if they don't make a profit during their leisure time. Dr. Norman Vincent Peale has good advice for such business executives: "I would first advise meditation. Silence is the element in which great things fashion themselves. Secondly I would urge him to find peace and quiet by organization. Finally I would urge him to, at bedtime, try to mentally drop all activities. Don't worry about what didn't happen today or what will happen tomorrow."

• A working wife may overextend herself, by holding down a demanding daily job . . . and burdened with guilt, try to keep everything running smoothly at home too (including her husband, children, the house or apartment, and all meals). But in doing so, they run the risk of burnout.

A study of the Newspaper Advertising Bureau revealed that "by 1990, the proportion of American women (between the ages of eighteen and sixty-four) who work outside their homes will top 68 percent."

• A salesperson may overextend himself or herself, by shooting for too high a goal or prize.

Many companies offer their star salespeople all-expense-paid trips each year to sales conferences held at fabulous resorts. Not every sales person (even the better ones) can achieve such a prize. A sales manager may naturally try to motivate the members of his sales team to try for one or more such prizes, when it may be out of reach for some of them. This may result in an overextension of self and lead to burnout.

• A nurse may take on too many duties without getting enough backup support. The current shortage of nurses puts a heavier work load on today's working nurses.

To avoid burnout, a nurse should learn how much can be handled without undue stress or burden and draw the line at that point. What good is getting more work done, if it results in leaving you burned out . . . and unable to function effectively in your chosen vocation?

• A student may overextend by trying to maintain high grades and work at a part-time job too.

• A teacher may overextend by agreeing to do too much. A speech teacher in the Midwest let herself get talked into directing a school play. She shouldn't have done it. She wasn't up to the extra responsibility, but felt too much guilt to refuse the task. She burned herself out during that difficult year. Keeping up with her daily classes, the preparation, grading, student records, and rest of it . . . plus the rehearsals and extra work of directing the play . . . were just all too much.

A vital point to remember is that not everyone is alike: one person's level of endurance usually differs from another's. You *can* perhaps take on more work and responsibilities than another person, but most of us do have our breaking points.

OVERCOMING THE EFFECTS OF JOB BURNOUT

Once you have suffered from job burnout, you will want to know how to get over the effects of it. There are definite things you can do to rise above such burnout effects as fatigue, the feeling of helplessness, the loss of sleep, too much alcohol, a low energy level, frequent illness, not caring about anything, and an overall feeling of being emotionally drained.

Remember. You don't have to be a white-collar office worker to feel the effects of burnout. Mothers at home, volunteer workers, and self-employed people are all possible victims.

It is important to realize from the start that you are only one of millions of others who have become victims of job burnout. Many persons have risen above the effects of such burnout, and have learned to enjoy life, and you can do it too.

A PLAN OF ACTION TO OVERCOME BURNOUT

Here are some action steps and *specific* things Dr. Caprio and I suggest you can do to overcome the effects of job burnout:

1. Listen to the signals of your body. When your body tires, it lets you know it with a variety of clues. You can hardly drag through the day. Even the smallest physical activities seem to take a lot of energy. Your body is signaling to you at such times that it needs rest. By delaying the rest you need, you may well bring on an illness. If you should become ill, remain at home. Don't keep trying to work two jobs or put in your usual eight-hours (or twelve, fourteen, or sixteen) a day, in spite of your sickness. This may only result in making your illness worse.

2. Watch closely for any signs of stress, often reflected by an increase in smoking, the use of alcohol or caffeine, overeating, sleep problems, bitterness, anger, depression, or headaches.

Many people suffering from burnout believe they can get over what is bothering them by eating, drinking, or smoking more. It just isn't true.

3. Examine all areas of your life to see where you seem to be going beyond the call of duty. Start with your job or position first, asking yourself these questions:

- Am I too dedicated to my job, to the point where it's burning me out?
- Do I have a growing or complete lack of interest in my job?

- Do I take advantage of the chance for rest breaks in my work? If the answer is no, why not?
- When I'm asked to take on more work, do I know how to say no?

4. If you don't already have some *daily* exercise program for yourself, get one going without delay. Swim, jog, walk, ride a bicycle, or what have you. Don't overdo your amount of exercise on any single day. Start slow and build, or increase, your amount of exercise gradually. What does you the good is the regular habit of exercising in some sensible way that works well for you.

Jack Schaff, an expert on stress management, admits that most of us do get some exercise through our work: "Work is healthy for you. It is stimulating and provides exercise. The body is designed to do work. What is unhealthy about it is that we are being called upon more and more to do more—and do it more quickly, more efficiently in terms of cost."

Remember too that there are all sorts of mini-exercises you can do that help reduce stress. Here are some very effective and popular ones:

- Rest your eyes every hour or so by looking out a window at somethng far away. This offers contrast to your close-at-hand work and eases your eye muscles.

   If your work requires that you stand or sit for long periods of time, change your position enough to offer relief from tension in your legs or back. Thomas Wolfe, the famous author, reportedly wrote a lot of his material standing up and using the top of a refrigerator for a desk. He was a very tall man and found this a comfortable way to write, rather than to sit for such long periods of time at a desk.
- When you feel tension building, try some deep knee bends, stretches of your arms and legs, or lean your head back and roll it clockwise and then counter-clockwise. All of these little exercises reduce tension.
- A favorite of mine is to take off my shoes (after a long session at a desk), turn them over, and roll my feet over the soles. This really relaxes the muscles in the feet.

   Don't forget, too, that you can quickly transport yourself to other places such as high in the Rocky Mountains, to the Swiss Alps, to the French Riviera, a cool wet rainstorm in London, to big sky country in Montana, or wherever. You take these trips via the speed and courtesy of your own imagination. They can be quite refreshing for you.

5. Use the Ben Franklin method to discover what things are bugging you about your job. Make two columns on a sheet of paper. In one column, list the things you like and enjoy about your job. For the other column, list the negative aspects or items. The idea here is to zero in on what's keeping you uptight about your job. This method helps you cut off the source of job burnout at the pass. This list method may help you to at least focus on some of your job irritations and show a comparison (on paper) of the good and bad things about your work.

6. Try switching from three meals a day to five or six small ones that are high in protein. If your doctor okays it, get yourself on a vitamin supplement plan (vitamins C, B6, and B2).

7. If there is monotony on your job, think of ways to relieve it. If you don't have enough to keep you busy, the hours of the work day will creep by all too slowly. The right changes, or additions, to your day's schedule might easily solve this problem.

8. Deep breathing exercises, or periods, a few times a day also reduce stress and tension. You simply take five-minute break periods to inhale and exhale. This practice seems to help many people in stress-related positions. Requirements are a relaxed body position, a quiet place, and banishment of all extraneous thoughts from your mind.

9. Try to seek ways to develop more confidence in yourself plus the power to defeat burnout. The way to send burnout and its effects packing is to meet your frustrations head-on and become victorious over them. If you feel you need a change in your work, let your superior or employer know it. The John Hancock Mutual Life Insurance Company offers their employees training in all areas. If an employee wants a change, the company has three full-time career counselors available for discussion about it. This clearly prevents a worker from feeling "locked" into a job he or she has grown tired of.

10. Don't take work home with you in the evening or over the weekends (if at all possible). Find *new* ways to get it done during the course of the work week, or ask for more assistance. Taking work home with you can lead to your becoming a workaholic.

The Department of Health, Education and Welfare reported that 64 percent of all blue-collar workers and 57 percent of all white-collar workers were unhappy in their jobs in a recent year and would choose different routes if they had the chance again. Many of these unhappy workers will make a change, which may well end the effects of burnout and lead them into a happier future.

So as still another way to overcome the effects of burnout, you should give some thought to a complete career or job change. Dr. Caprio advises you not to worry about a late job change in your life. It's happening more and more these days. Why be miserable in your job, when a complete change might open up a whole new horizon for you?

One of the most useful and helpful tools for improving your life is to think ahead. Project yourself into the future. If you feel there is no way out of the job that is causing havoc in your life, due to the combined effects of burnout, think well about making a full change. Go into some entirely different area of work. It may take planning to do it and saving enough money to make the break, depending upon your own situation, but don't rule this option out.

A basic truth about Winston Churchill, and one of the secrets of his success, was the fact that he had the brains to think ahead. He was always looking into the future . . . and wondering what lay ahead. Even in 1943, he knew that Germany was beaten, whether it took one, two, or three more years to do it. The combined power of Britain and America was too great. But Churchill was already thinking of the future threat posed by the Russians.

If you know that your job will only continue to produce burnout for you, and that you will not be happy in the work six months or a year from now, devise a plan to make a complete change into some other area of the employment. This decision alone might not only save you from the continued effects of burnout; it could restore the enthusiasm and interest you once had in your daily job. Think well on it.

9

Enjoy Your Coffee Breaks, Lunch Hours, and Vacations

Happy is the person who likes his or her job and enjoys his work. Those who hate their work feel as if they are wasting their lives. Every day is a horrendous grind for such people. If you are one of those people, begin to change your life today.

The focus of this chapter is to encourage you to see the *good* things about your work and to fully enjoy the coffee breaks, lunch hours, vacations, and other more specific fringe benefits connected with your job.

Coffee Breaks

Ask yourself this question: Am I enjoying my work as much as possible? Coffee breaks, for example, are part and parcel of each day. You are entitled to these breaks, if it's the custom or tradition where you work. This is especially true if you work hard on the job and do your best to give a solid day's work for a day's pay.

As you no doubt discovered long ago, coffee breaks are refreshing. They rest your mind, eyes, and body. The elementary and higher grade schools still have recess breaks each day, as much for the teachers as for the students.

Here are some of the plus features and advantages of coffee breaks. When and if you should feel guilty for taking your fair share of such breaks, turn back to this chapter and look over the following:

- Coffee breaks offer the chance for a little exercise. Unless you take your breaks right in the office, or on the premises where you work, you have to get to the restaurant, coffee shop, or snack place. So this means that you're moving and thus getting some exercise.
- Coffee, tea, or juice breaks are refreshing. They help to restore some zip to the rest of your day. One very successful salesman takes three short breaks a day and claims they have helped him to achieve his goals. He rarely takes over 10 or 15 minutes for each break, but always allows time for them in his daily schedule.
- Coffee, tea, or juice breaks provide an opportunity to exchange ideas and opinions. For example, the president and other officers of a branch office insurance company may go on breaks with the agents and office staff. Effective sales managers know that sometimes a friendly chat over coffee helps to motivate a sales team more than an hour-long formal meeting. People are often more relaxed over coffee and may express themselves better than in formal meetings.
- Coffee breaks help to establish a feeling of esprit de corps. This development of team spirit is essential to increased productivity, as Japanese business leaders have shown.

Lunch Hours

While it's not considered fair play to take two-hour lunch breaks, it is cheating yourself to skip lunch entirely or take too short an amount of time. Not enough time for lunch often results in simply rushing through a meal so fast that you have indigestion the rest of the day. And there's more to lunch than just food.

Lunch hours are made to enjoy yourself. If you arrive at your place of work at 8:00 to 9:00, you've been at it from three to four hours by high noon. You need and deserve a nice lunch—not a quick sandwich at your desk or hurry-up-and-gulp-it-down bite— so you can get back on the job in 15 to 30 minutes.

Here are some additional plus advantages of lunch hours:

- Many a personal or business problem has been solved (or helped out at least) over lunch.
- Lunch hours relieve stress, tension, worries, and general uptight feelings. They help you to relax.

- Some workers (including executives) make time for a nap during their lunch hour break. Presidents John F. Kennedy and Lyndon Johnson often took a nap after lunch and claimed it helped them accomplish more during the rest of the day.
- Many job-holders and employees vary the place where they eat lunch from day to day. This adds variety and interest to your day. Try this yourself. Go somewhere different for lunch frequently, instead of the same place every day.
- Lunch hours offer the chance for a leisurely outdoor walk or stroll with an associate, colleague, or friend.
- Lunch can give you an opportunity to stop in a variety of stores or perhaps to browse in a good bookstore. So lunch hours can be a *fun* break too.

VACATIONS

The other day I asked the butcher who waits on me in a local supermarket where he was going on vacation. "I'm not taking a vacation this year," he replied. I was surprised to hear him say that. He works hard, and I'm sure it has been a long year for him. So I asked why he was skipping a vacation. "Everything is so expensive. I think I'll just stay at home and relax."

While it's true that most vacations do cost more these days, Dr. Caprio and I think it's still important for most job-holders to get away from it all once a year. Taking it easy at home just isn't the same thing. Money is saved, but you miss the benefit of a refreshing change of scenery.

There's something psychological about a vacation. It helps you mentally, as well as physically, to get away. Look at it this way. After a year on the job, you deserve a vacation providing some new sights, activities, different things to think about, and an overall general change in your routine. Dr. Caprio emphasizes that vacations are healthy for you.

Two good friends of mine recently returned from a marvelous three-week vacation. They had been practically everywhere in the last several weeks . . . on an airline's special "no limit" travel plan. This special plan allowed them to fly anywhere in the country for 21 days. My friends reeled off the exciting places they had visited; the "no limit" ticket itself inspired the trip, and they had a wonderful time.

Here are some more advantages and pluses of vacations:

- It's often possible to combine business with a partial vacation, assuming you must take care of such business. For example, you may attend a convention or trade show (there are hundreds of them throughout the year in all parts of the country) and then stay on for an extra week or two of vacation.
- Many vacations are really stimulating in unplanned or surprising ways. You take tours, meet new people, learn about other peoples, customs, and countries, eat different food, and return home with quite a variety of sights and sounds to remember. In new environments you can relax and "allow" enjoyable events to happen.
- You may well lose weight on your vacation, because you're more active or moving around a good deal. Every year after I've returned from my vacation, I discover that I've lost five or more pounds. This is an extra dividend from your vacation. And it's a very nice one.
- Vacations offer a chance to renew old friendships and to return to places you love. An Academy Award winning songwriter in Hollywood was inspired by a fabulous hilltop view in Hong Kong to write one of his best songs—"Love Is a Many-Splendored Thing." He drew on the memory of that unforgettable view of the Hong Kong harbor and city to create this most enduring song.
- Vacations are a direct opportunity for you to enjoy yourself and forget all the little hurts, worries, troubles, and difficulties which life throws in your pathway. Whatever happens in your life, it's helpful to know that once a year you can call your soul your own and take off on a vacation holiday. In other words, planning where you will go on your next vacation, and looking forward to it, can be a strong motivating force for you and serve as a real tonic.
- Vacations also give you the time and chance to express yourself in any number of creative ways. You can enjoy your hobby or sideline interest while vacationing, be it photography, painting, or nature study.

Remember these words of Marcia Sobel Fox, an expert on burnout: "At my previous job I didn't take lunch or any break. At the end of the month I just couldn't take anymore. If I had kept it up for a year, I would have been completely burned out."

Don't short-circuit or shortchange yourself. Coffee breaks, lunch hours, and vacations are part and parcel of the work experience. If you do your job to the best of your ability, you have a right to expect your fair share of lunch, coffee, and vacation breaks (not to mention other more specific fringe benefits). Don't skip them. Make the most of them. And above all, *enjoy* them all, for even as you experience them, they are fleeting.

10

Facing and Conquering
Loneliness or Depression

Loneliness is a barrier to happiness. You cannot hope to enjoy life, to enjoy yourself and be happy, if you suffer from self-pity associated with loneliness. Loneliness is a sympton of your unhappiness. It is self-induced.

The good news, confirms Dr. Caprio, is that loneliness can be cured with self-analysis, self-education and self-therapy. To cure anything, it helps to understand that which you are trying to cure. Many people have misconceptions about what constitutes loneliness. Can you be married, for example, and still be lonely? Yes. Can you be in a crowd and feel alone? Yes. Does boredom constitute loneliness? Yes. Is loneliness associated with feelings of insecurity? Yes. The questions you could ask are endless.

The first step is to educate yourself regarding what we all agree is a liability—something that is self-defeating. What have psychiatrists learned about the type of person who complains of being lonely? He or she:

- Makes a habit of feeling isolated from others.
- Blames circumstances for the unhappy situation.
- Turns opportunities away for making friends.
- Wallows in self-pity and indulges in negative thinking about him or herself.
- Feels rejected.
- Is afraid to enjoy himself, easily bored, and lacks imagination.

The above are only a few of the many characteristics of the lonely. We have all met people at one time or another who complain of moods of depression, because of not having friends and not enjoying themselves. Loneliness today is a common malady, one that accounts for so much unhappiness. It's tragic because these same people could be enjoying themselves, if they were to assume a more positive attitude toward life and make an effort to cure themselves of their negative feelings.

It is estimated that one person in ten is living a life without benefit of friendships and companionship. It gives you some idea of how many people are depriving themselves of the happiness in life they could be enjoying. Instead they seem to prefer to be unhappy in their involuntary solitude. Because of this fact, people need to learn how to make the most of their short lifespan and find joy in the enjoyment of life.

Lonely people cannot hope to enjoy themselves, if they are at odds with themselves. Self-love is essential for the cure of loneliness.

The authors of this book recommend that you take an inventory of your personality. If you are super-critical, people will fear and avoid you. But if you radiate warmth and cheerfulness, people will be drawn to you. *You will never be lonely* if you show people you *care* about them.

"The loneliest people in the world," says Dr. Caprio, "are those who concentrate on themselves." As soon as you are interested in other people and other things, you won't be thinking about yourself. And when you aren't thinking about yourself, you cannot be lonely. In fact, it is impossible to be lonely when you are not thinking about yourself.

In order to be lonely, you must be telling yourself: "I am alone. I am lonely." Only when you start to feel sorry for yourself can you feel the symptoms of loneliness.

Give yourself a session of self-communication. Convince yourself of your own worth. Develop a positive image of yourself.

Actually, you need two things to banish loneliness from your life forever. One is a feeling of being important, and the other is a feeling of being wanted. Something that makes you feel worthwhile will give you this important feeling. To feel wanted, offer your help and services and friendship until people get accustomed to you and start wanting you.

In your conversation, have something to talk about besides yourself.

Be generous. The people who get left out are frequently those who do not share, do not contribute, do not carry their own weight. It does not matter what you give as long as you are a giving person.

Approach people as if they were already your friends. Lonely people act either shy or bitter, as if they are sure they won't be liked or already know they are not liked.

To make friends you must do the opposite. You must show with your smile and your own attitude of friendly interest that you already consider the other person to be a friend. You have accepted him or her. If you act standoffish, suspicious, secretive or frightened of people, they will avoid you because they will not feel sorry for you. And very few will make the effort to seek you out in friendship.

Overcome loneliness by keeping yourself busy. Gain confidence through accomplishments. Set up goals to work for. Never stop learning. Keep growing.

Try to understand and help others in distress, and you won't have time to feel sorry for yourself. Your kindness and the love you extend will be returned a thousandfold. If you give all the love that is possible for you, and accept the love of the world, your own happiness and enjoyment of life will be assured and the consequences of loneliness will vanish.

Natalie Prager made it clear that she has never allowed herself to become lonely, because she considers loneliness an *illness* which she avoids by keeping her mind and body active. She was always too busy to be lonely.

Natalie founded an organization called Welcome Visitors Show Stoppers. She has put new life into people who were professional entertainers, who rarely left their dingy hotel rooms in the west side area of Manhattan, because they lacked confidence in their ability to perform and, having little money, had no place to go.

Natalie also says that Welcome Visitors carries on extensive telephone visiting. "We call this Phono-Friends, and we make lonesome people very happy, who would otherwise be completely ignored by the passing throng. We also have Operation Cheer Card, and we send holiday greetings to hundreds of shut-ins— people who are old and alone."

How to Snap Back from Mental Depression

As a walking, breathing, living human, you have had and will have your share of depression. Most of us experience such depression from time to time, but the important thing is being able to snap out of it. Then *you* remain in control and when hit with depression you can always send it packing.

The causes of depression, or the blues, are numerous and varied. One reason for it may simply be the fact that it runs in your family. Some families do have a past history of certain kinds of depression.

Some types of depression require medical care, mood-elevating drugs, and psychiatric observation. Severe and endogenous depressions cannot be self-treated or cured by positive thinking and to attempt it may delay proper treatment.

Insults or rudeness can certainly cause a feeling of the blues. Who likes to be treated rudely or insulted? There are probably people walking around today still smarting from some insult or unkind remark they received years ago. The old cliché of "forgive and forget" is beyond the ability of these persons. They hear the insult over and over in their minds and can't seem to let go of it.

Disappointments can play havoc with your emotional state, unless you know how to deal with them. The idea is to be able to stay in control whenever you're disappointed about something. An excellent way to counter disappointment is to recall mental pictures of situations or events when you were victorious. You have met and conquered disappointments in the past and will do so many times again. No single disappointment or series of them can ever really knock you out of the ball game. Learn to react this way, and you can laugh at so-called disappointment, or at least weather the storms of life.

Other symptoms and causes of depression include the loss of ambition, less interest in what's happening around you and in the world, hostile feelings, possible damaging effects of one's early childhood days, the after-effects of diseases, drugs, tranquilizers, and basic temperamental changes. According to authorities on the subject, all these causes and others can bring on depression. The commonest cause of suicide today is depression.

Still another cause of depression is being rejected. Servicemen in the Armed Forces who received "Dear John" letters knew the very real feeling of rejection. What made it even harder was getting such goodbye-and-good-luck letters while out in the middle of nowhere, or just before leaving on a dangerous military mission. In these cases, unless those involved were able to snap back quickly (and get their bearings again), their very lives may have been, and probably were, much more endangered.

1. You can seek expert medical help if you wish. If depression is unusually severe or recurrent, consult your physician promptly. New drugs and skilled professional treatment can work miracles in some cases of severe or chronic depression. Your physician can refer you to specialists in the treatment of depression. If suicidal thoughts or impulses occur frequently, medical treatment must not be delayed.
2. You can try to handle it yourself.

One of the most effective ways to land back on your feet, when depression engulfs you, is to read some inspirational or positive material. Humorous items, cartoons, jokes, books, and magazines can also help.

Above all, remember that depression itself cannot cut you down but how you react to it can. Refuse to fight it, or welcome it by letting your mind dwell on it, and you're about licked already. But be determined not to let it take over your life and watch how soon the blues depart for weaker, more receptive minds.

You are the captain of your own mind and body. You and you alone decide what you'll think and how you'll react to any given event. Within this truth lies your power to drive away depression and keep it away.

SOME FOUR-STAR CURES FOR LONELINESS AND DEPRESSION

1. Spend an evening with a new and exciting book.
2. Write to some friends in distant states or countries.
3. Go through your attic, closet or storage space. You'll find all kinds of forgotten treasures.
4. Get outdoors and close to nature. Hike a few miles. Regular physical activity, especially walking and jogging, is often a sure cure.

5. Buy a puppy or kitten and raise it. You might even train your dog to do tricks.

6. Make plans for the next party or get-together with neighbors or friends.

7. Start a brand-new hobby—something you've always wanted to do, make, or study.

8. Decide on some sideline business you might be interested in and could devote time to on weekends or evenings during the week.

9. Make a list of what you would like to accomplish during the next three months.

10. Learn to play something on the piano or guitar. Or take up some other musical instrument.

11. Plan where you'll go on your next vacation and start collecting travel brochures on it.

12. Go to a concert or lecture on a subject that interests you.

13. Browse for a few hours in a good bookstore.

14. Complete and send in your entry for a contest or sweepstakes prize.

15. Create a story. Everyone has one story worth telling.

11

Make Enjoyment of Yourself a Major Goal

"The great purpose of life is to live it," said Oliver Wendell Holmes.

Self-happiness and enjoyment of life come from sharing your joys with others. The kindness and love you project return a thousandfold. This partnership with the rest of mankind is the great privilege of all of us. In it resides true happiness. When you develop strong ties with the world outside yourself, your own enjoyment is assured.

A positive effort to enjoy life, including yourself, stems from certain convictions that may be called collectively a "philosophy of life." The philosophy, according to Dr. Caprio, is based on the principle that happiness is an attitude which can be cultivated. It teaches you to expect sorrows and misfortunes, but at the same time gives you the courage to see them through. You owe it to yourself, your family, and your friends to win for yourself that measure of peace of mind—the right to enjoy life at any age.

Those who enjoy *themselves* the most are those who radiate cheerfulness, kindness and understanding. They possess a lovable disposition, and their philosophy of love sustains them even under adverse circumstances.

So why not make it your goal in life? Improve yourself in every way. Make self-improvement and the enjoyment of yourself a lifetime habit.

It would stagger your imagination to estimate the number

of people, perhaps millions, who don't know how to enjoy themselves. Many of them attribute their alleged inability to enjoy themselves to the fact that they are unhappy for one reason or another. There are others who are unable to understand the cause of their unhappiness and therefore do nothing about it. To enjoy *yourself* you need to learn to like or love yourself—to love life. To enjoy yourself here on earth should be one of the most important aspects of your life. Don't postpone happiness for the afterworld.

If you love life and yourself, you will be less apt to suffer from psychosomatic ailments. A positive self-image is basic to good health and happiness.

Masochism (a neurotic need to suffer and be unhappy because of guilt feelings or any other reason) is contrary to intelligence and common sense. Asceticism and martyrdom are products of sick thinking. The deliberate denial of healthy pleasures is not compatible with wisdom. You have *a right* to enjoy the pleasures of life, and the love of life must come from within. To enjoy yourself it is necessary for you to develop a feeling of self-acceptance. When you stop loving yourself, you stop loving someone else.

LOVE YOURSELF TO ENJOY YOURSELF

Love means the capacity to develop self-happiness. Happiness is the *mastery* of unhappiness. The need to love is present in all of us. Self-love is indispensable to enjoying yourself. Self-love is the absence of self-hatred. Deep down within each of us exists love-power that can make you live a fuller and more enjoyable life.

Dr. Caprio believes that if you love yourself, you are capable of loving others. If you hate yourself, you're unable to enjoy yourself. To expect love from others, you need to make yourself lovable.

Again, a positive self-image is the key to enjoying life. To enjoy yourself, channel your thinking to positive thoughts. Your future depends on your inner self, the way you think of yourself. The future is yours, to plan and to enjoy. To enjoy yourself requires a right attitude toward yourself—an attitude of believing in yourself. Believe that life is what you make it.

THE FULFILLMENT OF YOUR GOALS
BRINGS ENJOYMENT

In my youth I saw on the front of a building these words: "Plan your work. Work your plan." I was encouraged to believe that if a person wanted anything badly enough and planned for it, making it the most important thing in his or her life, he would improve his chances of getting it.

For many years, I had wanted to take a trip around the world, believing that this would prove a valuable investment for me. It would give me the opportunity of seeing how other people live, and would give me the kind of visual education I could never attain from books alone. I decided to make it one of the goals of my life. I chose, as my way of getting the necessary money for such a trip, to write articles and books after office hours and to start a separate savings account for the trip.

Years later, the plan materialized. I was not only happy knowing that I was taking the dream trip of my life, but a publisher offered me a contract to write a book that required traveling to foreign lands. The book was written and published, and I am planning another trip made possible by the royalties it earned for me.

Other goals may be accomplished in the same way—planning and then working out the plan. But the most important thing of all is to make the particular goal so vital that nothing is allowed to interfere with its accomplishment.

There is no question that the fulfillment of your individual goals is one way of enjoying yourself during your life.

A Hobby as a Source of Enjoyment

One of the best assurances for enjoyment in your life is the development of one or more interesting hobbies. Getting interested in something quite outside your regular work can do wonders. You'll be amazed to see what an uplifting effect it has on you and how much it adds to your personal enjoyment.

What kind of hobby it is doesn't matter much. Just so it interests you. Incidentally, in choosing a hobby, look to the future. Try to find something that not only absorbs you at the present moment but also holds promise of continuing interest. Adopt a hobby that will bring a full measure of enjoyment and interest as long as you live.

The point is that your hobby should be something in which you are honestly interested . . . something that hopefully is big enough to absorb every ounce of vitality and interest you can put into it, something that will grow as you yourself develop, becoming more fascinating with every passing year. This may be a rather tall order for the general run of hobbies. You may enjoy your hobby and get a great deal of pleasure from it, but still not be quite that interested. There's no reason at all to drop any hobby that is giving you even a little satisfaction. Hold on to it. But also consider taking up another one that may bring you far more enjoyment.

Above all, the important thing is to have a plan—one that meets your needs and desires. Then follow your plan consistently. Only in this way can you be sure of leading a truly satisfying and enjoyable life.

Immortal actor Edward G. Robinson started a hobby of collecting art from a $2.00 picture he bought in 1913. From that beginning, he built one of the country's best private collections. Edward G.'s first purchased picture was that of a fat cow, and he always liked to look at the cow, bad rendition though it was. "I never thought when I bought her, that life would come to this. I love my paintings. I have spent more for them than I can afford. But their ownership entails a definite obligation to share them with others."

ENJOY EVERY DAY

Think of life as one big cake. We inherit its ingredients and recipe at birth, mix it in childhood, bake it during adolescence, cover it with icing between the ages of thirty and fifty and enjoy it after fifty.

You can double your enjoyment of yourself, merely by adopting a positive mental attitude toward yourself and the world around you.

Sit down and work out a schedule of your usual week. Determine what times or days of the week you seem to be unhappy or not enjoying yourself. Then plan new and special periods of enjoyment for those times. I discovered, for example, that early Saturday afternoons were often gloomy for me. I did something about it. I now drive to one of the large shopping malls (either with a friend or alone) and spend part of the afternoon. It has worked wonders. I enjoy going through the stores, browsing in the bookstores, and ending up my visit to the mall with a chocolate soda or coke float in one of the snack or ice cream places.

Dare to dream again. To dream, to learn, to think, to work, and to laugh. These should constitute the basis of your new philosophy of life.

12

The "Lost" Art
of Enjoying Sex

Sex for many people has only the connotation of a physical act. Sexuality, on the other hand, should connote an expression of your total personality, *a special form of communication*. Sexuality entails a need to enjoy yourself, to love, give love and share love. It involves your total self, your total ego. It is synonymous with a *body-soul communication*. In lovemaking you are making love with your mind as well as your sex organs.

Dr. Caprio confirms that lovemaking is a science as well as an art. Your health, your marriage, your sexual fulfillment and your happiness are all dependent on the degree to which you understand what the sex-love relationship is and how to attain and use it. We all need to learn about sex. The healthy management of sex is essential to successful living. Sexual happiness is part of our total happiness in life.

Grappling with the complications of modern life, we sometimes forget the enormously important role sex plays in our personality and emotional well-being. Sex does not exist in an isolated compartment. Its effect permeates your entire life. An ability to enjoy mature sexual love depends on your capacity for every form of love and affection, and this in turn leads to better relationships with family and friends. It lends an inner poise that is communicated to everyone you meet.

As Dr. Ashley Montagu puts it, "Sex is the most wonderful thing in the world, and next to the love of a mother for her child, it is the most beautiful experience in relation to another person which any human being can enjoy."

Everyone is involved in one way or another with sexuality. Some participate and gratify their sexual desires. Others prefer to repress them, or they try to sublimate their pent-up sexual energy. To be realistic, you can't be "bottled up" sexually and not pay a price. To deny sex is to dehumanize yourself. Remind yourself that sexual fulfillment is an all-embracing body-mind experience. It adds to the joy of existence, or as the French say "joie de vivre."

As a person you have every right to sex-happiness—the right kind of course. The right to sex-happiness implies that which is not detrimental to yourself or others. It involves enjoying the love, the security and the peace of mind to which you are entitled.

Pleasurable sex must start with yourself. It begins with the right attitude toward sex. Many patients seeking sex therapy encounter major sex problems only because they didn't have the right attitude toward sex to begin with. They never realize that it is normal to enjoy sex, that it is normal to want to know more about sex, to read authoritative sex books and not fear what other people might think or say. You can't do anything well if you are blocked from the start.

If your mind is open, it will be receptive to the enjoyment of sex pleasures that will benefit you. Convince yourself that you have the capacity to enjoy sex. It means a healthier way of living and a greater capacity for love and happiness in marriage. Marriage should represent a reciprocal agreement to enjoy sex.

There is no blueprint for the enjoyment of sex. No two people are alike sexually. The common denominator of a good sexual relationship is a frankness between husband and wife. Compromise means better adjustment for both. Each has to make concessions to the other's needs. In order for them to enjoy sex, they must be honest with each other. There should be frank requests for what is needed for maximum pleasure.

Dr. Hyman Spotnitz and Lucy Freeman, free-lance writers, contend that sex occupies an important aspect of our total happiness: "Sex should be part of our lives, not the whole of our lives. If we are unhappy sexually, no matter how happy we believe ourselves in other areas, we never feel fulfilled. But if we are happy sexually, we are usually also happy in the rest of living."

They add: "There is nothing sinful about pleasure. We all

need a proper amount of pleasure to get through life successfully. Pleasure to a human being is like oil to a machine; it lubricates our personality so we can function more easily. But if we live only for pleasure, it is as destructive as denying ourselves any pleasure at all."

This idea could not be expressed more effectively.

Sexual lovemaking is a science and an art which can be learned. Considering the abundance of published literature on the subject, there is no excuse for anyone to be uninformed in sexual matters.

SEX-UNHAPPINESS CAN BE PREVENTED

No one needs to feel guilty for wanting to be sexually fulfilled. Sex is a God-given gift, not man-made.

The number of men and women who are sexually unhappy runs into the millions. Our rapidly increasing divorce rate (the highest in the world) is an indication of the large number of couples who have experienced serious sex-love problems— serious enough to cause them to dissolve their marriages.

Sex-unhappiness also has a detrimental influence on your physical health. It accounts for numerous psychosomatic complaints such as tension, headaches, excessive chronic fatigue, depressed moods, vague aches and pains, insomnia, nervousness, and other troubles. Sex health can mean new vitality, a longer and more satisfying life, according to Dr. Caprio.

Fortunately, we are taking a healthier and more honest attitude toward sex and love. Progressive changes are taking place.

Sex-unhappiness need not exist. It can be prevented. It can be cured. Almost everyone can, with effort, develop the kind of sex-love relationship that makes for an ideal marriage and family happiness. It is a matter of self-education, of acquiring a new sense of values, of understanding the cause of your sex-unhappiness and doing something about it. Sex enjoyment is interrelated with health and love-happiness.

It is surprising how many men and women are sexually unhappy, who find it difficult to enjoy the sexual relationship, because they are troubled by conflicting moral attitudes involving sex and religion. The clergy, however, are beginning to appreciate the fact that sex-health is basic to happiness.

We are all born to enjoy a healthy love-sex life. It is the misuse of sex (and the complications we ourselves invite) that creates the conflicts between sex and religion.

The sex act between a man and a woman can represent the ultimate expression of love. It is part of the perfect love which is the source of all our joy in life. As an expression of love between a man and a woman, it renews their instinct to love, to survive disaster together and to *enjoy* life.

RECOMMENDED WAYS TO DEVELOP SEX-HAPPINESS

Here are some specific recommendations to develop sex-happiness, to achieve greater sexual satisfaction and contentment:

The first step is to dispel whatever fallacies you harbor about sex. It is essential that you start out with a healthy attitude about sex in general. You must believe that it can be fun and pleasurable. It can be a source of happiness. This you must repeat to yourself over and over again.

There are many things a good husband-lover can do to help his wife achieve sexual satisfaction. Foreplay is necessary for most women to become properly aroused. A woman's ability to achieve a sexual climax also depends on her attitude toward intercourse, her ability to concentrate, the extent of her wanting to enjoy intercourse, and her talent for abandoning herself completely to the pleasurable sensations of the sex act.

Some experience an intensity at the peak of the sexual act. Others experience one orgasm after the other from the first intromission until the act is completed. Orgasms can become more enjoyable with experience and experimentation.

Experienced lovers know that there are various movements that add to the ecstasy of the sex act. By practicing these different movements, uninhibited lovers can achieve a certain amount of proficiency in the art of lovemaking.

An occasional change in techniques tends to make sex more enjoyable and satisfying. By experimenting with various positions, you experience a variety of physical sensations.

Husbands and wives should make time for a reasonable amount of afterplay. The expression of affection and tenderness after the sex act gives the relationship a deeper significance. A wife can reaffirm her satisfaction in the course of her husband's afterplay, by telling him how happy he has made her. Husbands must remind themselves that sexual excitement in women abates gradually. Therefore he must not be too abrupt in terminating the lovemaking. Following satisfactory sex relations, both husband and wife should experience a sense of complete relaxation, fulfillment and contentment.

For sex to be enjoyable, couples should manifest a warmth, spontaneity, and above all imagination. Variations in sex technique have the advantage of making sexual relations more pleasurable. Sex variety and experimentation are both healthful and proper.

Every couple should strive to develop a technique in lovemaking which will result in the greatest amount of mutual satisfaction. Artful lovemaking can lead to indescribable bliss.

Many people past fifty commit so-called sexual suicide. They become sexual dropouts. They think they are too old to enjoy sex. They fear that they may prove inadequate and deliberately try not to think about sex. Their spouses may be too inhibited to mention the matter, and before long the marriage begins to deteriorate, apparently for reasons unknown to either partner. Sex need not stop with the passing years. If you keep sex and love alive in your mind, nature will surprise you. You will find that you are more adequate than you thought you would be. Attitude is tremendously important where sexual longevity is concerned.

The longevity of your sex life runs parallel to the longevity of your *enthusiasm* for living. When life becomes monotonous, sex becomes monotonous. As Havelock Ellis, world-famous sexologist wrote, "Sex has a tendency to die in the middle years, but only in couples who are unimaginative and where sex has become routine."

Statistical facts indicate that aging couples are capable of enjoying themselves sexually. The secret is to keep young in heart. Keep the warmth and closeness alive in your marriage. The kiss, the clasp of hands, the embrace—these are the gestures of a sex-love partnership. They should never be abandoned.

13

How to Enjoy Marriage

Another title for this chapter could well be, "The Secret of a Happy Marriage." But the word "secret" should be plural. There's more than one secret to a happy and enjoyable marriage, as you will discover.

Whatever the secrets of a successful and enduring marriage are, they involve the lives of two human beings. When a man and a woman pledge their vows, they're in effect entering into what for many years was believed to be one of life's greatest adventures. In recent years, however, marriage has lost much of its allure, respect, and esteem. Millions of young couples have lived openly together, after voicing their conviction that "marriage kills off the love between a couple."

But authorities on marriage believe that the closing decades of this century will paint a different marriage picture. Marriage is going to make a tremendous comeback. That comeback has already begun. Once again, it's going to be the "in thing" to be married. An enormous new respect for marriage, and the desire to be married, will be evident once again.

Dr. Joyce Brothers, the well-known psychologist and marriage authority, predicts more durable marriage relationships for the rest of the century. She feels there will be fewer "panic marriages" in which girls decide to marry because they've reached a certain age. More care in choosing a marriage partner will also prevent adultery and divorce. "Women's new freedom makes them less apt to marry for wrong reasons, and those marriages which do take place should be happier and more rewarding for both partners."

HAPPINESS IS A WORKING WIFE

Some say that the happy and enjoyable marriages are those in which the wife is a working woman. Others disagree. With the rising cost of everything in this last part of the century, the majority of couples have little choice. It has become a necessity in a great many marriages for the wife to hold down a job.

It is true that numerous wives have tried to keep both a career and marriage going smoothly. But in many cases, their marriages have shown signs of trouble and strain. Yet there are plenty of other women who seem to be running both their jobs or careers and marriages successfully.

Not only is marriage going to be very popular again in the coming years, but staying married will be most important as well. Millions of new couples will want to stay married. Young men and women who don't marry during this new marriage boom (which is on the way) will feel very much out of style.

The extra money earned by today's working wife, and the help she brings to the family, may be a prime reason why a lot of marriages will last . . . why couples will choose to stay married.

STAYING IN TUNE WITH YOUR MARRIAGE PARTNER

Aside from the fact that most couples share in the work routine these days, by holding down jobs, what are some other ways to stay in tune with your marriage partner? Here are some proven pointers and suggestions Dr. Caprio and I recommend that have helped many couples to stay close and to get more enjoyment from their marriages:

1. Find and maintain a mutual interest you can share. A major reason for the happy and successful marriage of the Irving Wallace family is their work. The Wallaces have a mutual interest. Both Sylvia and Irving are writers, as are their children Amy and David. This shared interest in writing has certainly paid off for the Wallaces in more ways than one. As Irving admits, "Work-

ing together has kept us very close. I've learned a great deal about Amy and David, and Sylvia too, through their writing."

2. Cut down on the amount of time you watch television. If you can manage to do this, it will help your marriage. A number of couples are even shutting off their television sets for good, or moving the one-eyed monster out of their homes entirely. Many of these couples claim that no television in the house or apartment has increased the harmony of their marriages. They simply *communicate* more with their mates, without the distraction of television. As one woman put it, "Television is an idiot box. People are dumb and boring who watch it, or they are old and can do nothing else but sit."

If you and your spouse like certain favorite programs on the tube, you could of course simply watch those and ignore the rest of the offerings. The choice is up to you.

3. Be ready and willing to give 75 percent of yourself, whether you get that much in return from your mate or not. This may of course be a tall order for some persons.

Keep in mind that you must do a combination of things to stay in tune with your marriage partner. It's not any ONE thing by itself. Harmonious and more enjoyable marriages are usually those unions characterized by unselfishness, kindness, understanding, consideration of each other's interests, hobbies, goals, and dreams, plus a strong basic respect for the thoughts and feelings of each other.

I asked twenty-five different married people recently what they felt was the single most important quality needed for a successful and harmonious marriage over the years. The answer kept coming up over and over, although the words varied. The majority of the couples said the same thing: "The single most important quality is that you have to be willing to give more than you get."

4. Strive continually to improve yourself as a person and your overall personality. Being a good person is, in itself, part and parcel of the secret of a happy marriage.

I know a couple now in their late thirties who prove that this continuous goal of self-improvement really works. Both wife and husband have increased their self-knowledge and marital adjustment to a considerable degree. Both of them seek to show their love for each other in little unexpected ways. The wife, for example, showed her unselfishness and love for her husband, Tom, by secretly saving money for over eight months to buy him an expensive camera he had long wanted. They are devoted to each other and to keeping their marriage an unusually happy one over the years ahead.

Unfortunately, too many young couples get married with the belief that they are both just about perfect and know all there is to know. So by starting out with this kind of attitude, they have no way to go but the wrong way. Their marriage deteriorates because they have little or no desire for self-improvement.

5. Try to be realistic regarding the expectations for your marriage. If your expectations are too high, you may be disappointed. Few marriages can live up the "happily ever after" myth.

Realize the difference between loving and "being in love." As C. S. Lewis put it, "It is this other, quieter love that enables two people to keep their promise. It is on this love that the engine of marriage is run. "Being in love" was merely the explosion that started the engine."

6. Pre-marital counseling according to Dr. Caprio, will help to make your marriage a successful and lasting one. In these meetings, both the man and woman learn the importance of striving for an open and honest communication in their marriage. Getting your marriage off in the right way can only improve its chances for success.

7. If you have a tendency to buy too many things with a credit card, start leaving your card (or cards) at home. Money issues head the list of conflicts in far too many marriages.

A bankrupt is "a person legally declared unable to pay his or her debts." To obtain this declaration, one must file a specific bankruptcy petition with a federal court clerk and pay a filing fee. Any property owned by said person is divided among the creditors.

According to research on this subject, "About ninety percent of all bankrupts are married. The reason is that marriage brings with it extra money problems. The typical husband's income does not go up, but the number of bills does. More and more credit is used until couples find themselves in a nightmare of debt.

8. Whatever problems confront you and your mate, decide to face them together. By meeting them together, little or

no damage will be done to your marriage. In fact, your marriage will be strengthened. Marriage means sharing the hard times (if any) as well as the good ones. Most marriages encounter some lean years over a long period of time so it helps a great deal to be determined not to let them wreck your marriage.

9. Avoid arguments on what each of you "wants out of life." Such arguments can develop into a stalemate. Try to find a mutual ground on which both of you can agree regarding future goals. What do you *enjoy* together?

10. Find some way to compliment your mate every day. One of the major causes of tension in a marriage is the neglect of courtesies and compliments. Everyone likes to feel that he or she is appreciated. This includes your not forgetting birthdays and anniversaries.

11. Go off somewhere together at least a few times a year. If possible, take a short trip once every six weeks or quarter. Have fun together planning where you'll go and working out the details. This gives you both something to look forward to. The change of scenery and different routine for awhile (if only over a weekend) will ease tensions and give you both a fresh viewpoint. You'll come back home renewed.

12. Kiss each other goodbye each morning when the day's work separates you, or when you both leave for the jobs you hold. These little opportunities to show affection are very important for a happy marriage. Don't fail to express love and appreciation that is due.

13. Bring your spouse a little gift now and then, have dinner out together and enjoy some special entertainment.

14. Plan one of your favorite meals (or dishes) occasionally. This will be difficult, of course, if you're a working couple, because you'll be pressed for time and tired when you get home from work. But there's always Saturday and Sunday as possible times to experiment with a new recipe. Why not cook a meal together? Many couples take turns with the cooking, surprising each other with exciting meals.

15. Go dancing together now and then, and choose a place where at least a good portion of the music provided is smooth and romantic.

One of the best things to happen for couples everywhere,

married or not, is the return of close-up dancing. The years when everyone did a solo on the dance floor are about over, we hope.

One of the very best places to go dancing in the Midsouth area, for many years, was the Peabody Hotel Skyway, in Memphis, Tennessee. But the name band era ran its course, and the famous Peabody Hotel was closed. Several attempts to reopen it failed. But now the hotel has been restored to its charm and grace, it's open, and at this writing, the Peabody is booking fine dance bands on a regular basis. Couples in the Mid-south area now have a marvelous place to go dancing once more.

Close-up dancing is getting popular again, and it's high time. It will provide a most enjoyable evening once more for a lot of couples. Above all, it will put more romance back in millions of lives. That's exactly what a great many marriages need badly today—more romance.

Barbara Cartland, the famous London romance novelist, was right when she said that the royal wedding opened up a lot of eyes and made millions of couples realize how much they need more romance in their lives. As Barbara put it, "Millions of people everywhere have realized how starved they are for romance. The whole world is crying out for romance."

16. Have room in your home life for religion. You know how the saying goes: "The family that prays together stays together."

In a questionnaire sent out my a minister to over 750 couples he had married, this question was asked: "What in your judgment is the greatest element making for happiness in home life?" The largest number of replies said "religion lived daily in the home."

The above ideas and suggestions are not the only recommended ones for a happy marriage. But they will definitely help to cement your marriage and make it a more *enjoyable* one.

May your marriage be one of the enduring ones. And may it lead you and the one you love to new vistas of enjoyment and happiness.

14
Take Time for Everything

Southern hospitality is legendary. Some Danish visitors found this certainly to be true, when they stayed with a family in Virginia during a tour of the United States. The Danes were so pleased that they presented their American hosts with a unique gift from Copenhagen: a hand-embroidered scroll. On it was neatly stitched "Take Time for Everything," followed by a list of nine ways people can enjoy themselves. The Virginians hung the scroll in their family library, and it became a daily reminder of how we should take time for the important things in life, basic wisdom on how to truly enjoy life:

TAKE TIME FOR EVERYTHING

1. Take Time to Work.
   It is the price of success.
2. Take Time to Think.
   It is the source of power.
3. Take Time to Read.
   It is the fountain of wisdom.
4. Take Time to Dream.
   It is hitching your wagon to a star.
5. Take Time to Be Friendly
   It is the road to happiness.
6. Take Time to Love and Be Loved.
   It is the privilege of the gods.

7. Take Time to Play.
    It is the secret of perpetual youth.
8. Take Time to Look Around.
    It is too short a day to be selfish.
9. Take Time to Laugh.
    It is the music of the soul.

TAKE EACH DAY AS IT COMES

You've heard it before, but it's well worth repeating. Don't live in the future. And don't live in the past either. The only chance you have to be *happy* is to take each day as it comes, do your best, and make up your mind to be happy . . . as happy as possible. Live in the present. Yesterday is gone forever, and tomorrow may never come. The only thing you have and can be sure of is today. So make the most of each priceless day. Dr. Caprio suggests that you copy the above nine time statements and follow them.

Some people have to literally force themselves to climb into bed at night. They see the time spent resting each night as time down the drain. They find it hard to take time for sleep, as important and needed as it may be. The human body has to be renewed of course, but look at all that time that gets used up while you're out of the picture. Composer Jerome Kern hated to go to sleep at night. He got many of his best melody ideas at night, so he often stayed up and worked. This is also true of many other creative thinkers. They are night owls. There has been some scientific study of this fact.

Perhaps the best way to handle the years you and I have—that go by like a whirlwind—is simply to try to get more out of each day. There's no exact rule that says you absolutely must get eight or nine hours of sleep every single night. Maybe you could occasionally get up an hour earlier or stay up an hour or two later, devoting the extra time to reading, recreation, or just thinking. Time is even more valuable than money.

HOW TO GET MORE OUT OF YOUR TIME

You may now have a regular plan for your free time. And you may have already worked out the goal or goals you wish to reach through constructive use of your time, whether it is a few hours a week or many. If you haven't done any such planning, begin today. Better use of your time will enable you to live fuller, happier days. Learning how to take time for the things you want to accomplish and enjoy will bring you more satisfying fulfillment. Here are some proven guidelines for getting more out of your time:

1. Review each night what you can do to get more done during each day. Think about a way you can salvage more time and put it to better use. Write down the ideas you get and then put them into action.

2. Make your lunch hours count more. You would be surprised at how many people take two hours or more to enjoy lunch. It may not look like much time over a few days or weeks, but six months or a year of long lunch hours add up to a lot of time.

Years ago, a well-known composer and pianist was trying to develop his skill at playing the piano. He was good at the piano, but he wanted to improve much more. He found a piano he could use during his lunch hour and started practicing on it for at least half of his usual lunch time. He did this for many months and said that the extra practice he got in really added up and helped him to become an excellent pianist. He took the time he needed for extra practice, even though it meant giving up half his lunch hour. In his view, it was well worth it.

3. Get by on less sleep (if you can do so without hurting your health). This is one more way to find time for all you want to do. Just devote less time to your shut-eye. Millions of people do get by quite well on six or seven hours of sleep a night. The great inventor Thomas Edison often slept only four hours at a stretch, but he did take short naps when he felt tired.

4. Plan more interesting things to do, places to go, and sights to see during your weekends.

Your weekends offer some wonderful time for hobbies, gardening, travel, or any number of interests. But it takes planning to get more out of them. If you don't do some advance thinking and planning, it will be Sunday night faster than you might realize . . . leaving you possibly disappointed that you didn't take the time to do more (or make better use of the weekend that was). Take five and add up how many hours 52 weekends a year figures out to be. That's a lot of valuable time for you to enjoy all kinds of things.

5. Study the methods of those who have somehow found the time to do a lot and achieve a great deal.

A study of various people from all walks of life, and how they were able to get so much done with their time, can be a great help to you. Why? Because you can sometimes apply the same method or idea yourself.

BE TRUE TO YOURSELF

Shakespeare said it well: "To thine own self be true." One almost sure way to discover whether you must take the time to do certain things is to project yourself five, ten, or more years into the future. Then ask yourself if you'll be able to live with yourself at that point in time, knowing that you still haven't done the things you wanted to do.

Here are some questions that will help you to determine if you are taking the time to get more out of life:

		Yes	No
1.	Have I taken the time to do some (or all) of the things that I feel are important to me?	_____	_____
2.	Do I take some time each day to dream about what I would like to do, become, achieve, or enjoy during my life?	_____	_____
3.	Do I take the time to plan ahead so I don't spin my wheels on things or projects that are not important to me?	_____	_____
4.	Do I take the time to keep in touch with old friends and to try to make new ones whenever possible?	_____	_____
5.	Do I take the time to relax a little each day and simply enjoy being alive?	_____	_____

Give yourself twenty points for each "yes" answer and then add up your total. This will give you a good idea of whether time is slipping by in your life, without you getting your share of enjoyment from it.

15

Questions and Answers
to Guide You

The following are some of the most frequently asked questions about the pursuit of enjoyment. The answers that follow are meant to offer you further guidance along your own road to more enjoyable living:

Q. *Wouldn't a shorter work week, and the extra free time it would mean, bring more enjoyment to many people?*

A. It would indeed. An increasing number of executives and employees are convinced that a four-day work week should be set as the standard routine. For several years now, about 3,000 American companies have been on the four-day schedule on a regular basis. The total number of workers involved is over a million. So the idea of a four-day work week isn't all that new. There are two sides on the idea. Some have pointed out the negative aspects such as idleness causing an increase in crime, the longer time it would take to train newcomers on a job, more hours spent in front of television and other effects. The answer for many companies seems to be to try the idea out on an experimental basis and see how it goes.

Q. *How can I enjoy things in general when I'm unemployed?*

A. I see your point. I urge you to contact the Job Bank, which is a creation of the United States Employment Service. The Job Bank is computerized. It doesn't list every available job, but many of the largest employers use it when they're ready to hire new people.

The Job Bank is broken down into 200 geographic districts and includes some 45 different job characteristics listed by employers. As an example, in a recent month the Job Bank listed 350,000 jobs in about 125 different categories. More than half of these jobs were filled. The Job Bank will cost a whopping $822 million to operate this year. Here is the address of the United States Employment Service: 601-D Street, N.W., Washington, D.C., 20213.

Q. *What about daydreaming? Is it a waste of time?*

A. Not if you personally enjoy it. Millions of people around the globe engage in some degree of daydreaming almost every day. "Fantasy Island," the hit television series, was based on the human desire to daydream and fantasize about all manner of wishes and wants.

Q. *I paint pictures when I can find the time. I enjoy painting, but is it really worth it?*

A. It is indeed. And there's always the chance that your painting will become increasingly successful. Sheryl Bodily in Montana gave up the security of his job at a local sawmill to try his wings as a full-time professional artist. He could only work at his art after a full day on his job, but he went home each evening and immediately started to paint. Over a period of ten years, he added a great deal of skill and experience to his part-time painting. His evening efforts eventually blossomed into a full and successful career. This fulfillment has brought him great enjoyment: "All during the ten years I was painting and selling a few pieces, but not until shortly before I left my job did I believe I was ready to be a full-time artist."

Q. *Every morning when I wake up, I can't shake the feeling that it's going to be a bad day. How can I reverse this attitude and enjoy my days more?*

A. Take five minutes or so and force yourself (if necessary) to think only happy and enjoyable thoughts. This short saying has worked well for many. I urge you to repeat it any number of times each morning: "This day is going to be a happy, productive, and enjoyable one. I am sure of it."

Q. *Can you suggest something enjoyable to do at home while my family is not around?*

A. How about trying some small interior decorating projects? It's enjoyable to try some new curtains in certain rooms, to switch furniture around (although this can be heavy work if you go overboard on it), and bring a different look to some areas of your home or apartment.

Going through your attic or storage room can also be a surprisingly satisfying task. It almost always results in the finding of some treasures you forgot you had.

Q. *I would like to do something that is both enjoyable and creative on my day off. Do you have any ideas?*

A. One of the most enjoyable and creative activities is to try and dream up a brand new game—something fresh and different, as well as interesting or challenging. This is the very way the game Monopoly was born. A man stayed home one rainy afternoon and created this fabulous board game for his own amusement. The result was game history. Monopoly remains today one of the best-selling and most popular games of all time.

Q. *I know I would enjoy life more if I could quit putting so many things off. Can you help me?*

A. Maybe you need to set priorities more. Dr. Caprio advises to try choosing just a few important things to get done. Make a list each day of the urgent tasks you have to accomplish. Then reward yourself in some way for sticking to your purpose. The trick is to make this a habit. Then it gets easier to get important things done on a daily and weekly basis. This method does seem to work for many and leaves them with more time for their personal enjoyment.

By the way, it might be an enjoyable project for you to see what you could do about forming an organization called the National Society of Procrastinators. Your group could meet periodically and quite possibly develop into an interesting and enjoyable club.

Q. *Isn't the enjoyment of leisure the same as enjoying idleness?*

A. They aren't really the same thing. Leisure is thought of by most people as one's free time not spent on a job or in the pursuit of making a living.

Q. *What do you think of collecting something regularly . . . just for the enjoyment of it?*

A. Many are doing it these days. Collecting stamps, coins, buttons, dolls, books, posters, paintings, or whatever is one of the best ways to enjoy yourself. Some people who started a collection for the fun of it have also seen their collections grow to be very valuable.

Q. *Can you recommend something different to do at night, to keep me away from the television set?*

A. You might consider taking an evening course at a local college or university, or an adult education course at a local high school. A class that meets one, two or three times a week would be something different for you. Try to sign up for a course in a subject of real interest to you. Most colleges and adult education schools will be glad to provide you with their planned program for the regular term or summer session. You can then choose the courses that seem to be of most interest to you. Nearly every local community college offers a variety of courses, so you're certain to find some that you would enjoy. Many school districts now offer adult and continuing education programs for all ages, so you need not live near a large university.

Q. *Should I focus on just a few activities I enjoy, or go for the whole baker's dozen or more?*

A. If you have the time, it's great to enjoy a variety of interests, activities, and hobbies. But if you have a limited amount of time, it would be better to select the few pursuits that bring you the most enjoyment. Stick with them until you have more time to devote to additional activities.

Q. *Aside from my business, the only time I really enjoy myself is when I'm smoking. Does this mean that I'm not capable of further enjoyment?*

A. I don't think so. There are bound to be at least some other sources of enjoyment for you. Perhaps you haven't tried other routes to enjoyment (or enough of them), or maybe you've just been working too hard in recent years. Some people never seem to enjoy themselves simply because they can't *unwind* and relax.

Keep in mind that one of the five major factors that increase the risk of a heart attack is smoking a pack or more of cigarettes a day. Dr. Caprio and I urge you to cut out your smoking entirely, if at all possible.

Q. *I enjoy speaking to student, church, and civic groups in my area. Isn't speaking a good way for many people to increase their enjoyment?*

A. I agree with you myself. But the fact remains that a lot of people out there get panic-stricken at the mere thought of speaking before a small or large audience. I do think that thousands of adults and young people, too, could increase their enjoyment by developing their ability to speak to others. It is a challenging and fascinating way to spend some of your free time. Women's clubs, garden groups, student assemblies, and business or civic organizations (plus associations) all use speakers.

The plus feature of speaking is the triple value you get from it: (1) You enjoy expressing yourself to others and knowing that something you say may inform, entertain, or inspire members of an audience. (2) You meet a lot of interesting new people and also may enjoy travel to other cities and sections of the country. (3) You may well earn a handsome side income from speaking, if you develop enough skill, confidence, and experience. According to published reports, Senator Howard Baker earned $25,000 in speaking fees alone last year (in addition to his regular yearly salary). But many unknown speakers add considerably to their income by speaking before various groups on a variety of subjects. The fees for speaking will also continue to rise steadily through the rest of the century.

Q. *Wouldn't participating in a fan club be a possible way that many people might find enjoyment?*

A. The best answer I can give you is the thousands of devoted Elvis Presley fan club members spread all over the world. These members evidently derive an enormous amount of enjoyment and personal satisfaction, by remaining so loyal to the late king, as they still refer to him. Some 10,000 Presley fans made the journey to Memphis, Tennessee this year, in order to spend August 16 at the star's Graceland mansion. All of them stood by the grave of Elvis again and attended the several days of planned events in the city commemorating another anniversary of the singer's death. The Elvis fan clubs are quite active all year long in their various locations around the globe, and they seem to be very determined to keep the memory of Elvis alive and strong as the years go by.

16

Learn to Spice Your Life With Recreational Outlets

A world of enjoyment awaits you in a variety of recreational outlets, if only you can discover them and learn to make the most of them. It is largely a matter of fitting them into your routine or schedule.

Let's take a look at some of these recreational outlets and see how they can increase your enjoyment:

All-Day Outings

If and when you can get away for an entire day, an outing is one good choice of recreation open to you. A drive to a nearby town or park area makes an appealing one-day outing. You can have a picnic with friends, swim, fish, or hike. If there are attractive areas or towns nearer to where you live, you might be able to get back in less than a full day.

A busy insurance executive I know likes to drive to a national park area about twenty-five miles from his home. He enjoys hiking around and having lunch there. He says the break in his usual daily routine and the different surroundings help him to get some good thinking done. He takes off on these outings once or twice a month at least, sometimes staying for only half a day.

For many years, a married couple I knew in Indiana enjoyed driving to nearby small towns, having lunch, walking around the town, and often visiting friends in the various areas. They loved learning about the towns in that geographical area.

Since both of them were very busy during the week, Saturdays and Sundays were the usual times for their outings.

Exploration Trips

An all-day outing is merely an abbreviated version of a full exploration trip. The desire or itch to go exploring can be relentless. It appeals to your sense of adventure and newness, while being a four-star form of recreation at the same time.

Englishman John Merrill, an author of books about the countryside and a man in love with exploration (and long distance walking), spent some ten months walking around the coastline of England, Wales, and Scotland. His remarkable 7,000-mile adventure consumed, required, wore out, or used up the following items:

- Three pairs of boots
- Hundreds of gallons of milk
- 33 pairs of socks
- 1,000 bars of chocolate
- 60 pounds of equipment

Merrill met hundreds of people on his exploration walk and was interviewed by the local press and radio-television along the way. He began walking promptly at 8:30 each morning and quit for the day at 5:00. He was invited to a number of evening events, as he made the marathon journey.

Merrill's adventure not only resulted in his personal enjoyment of seeing the changing coastline; he put the story of his exploration, the events of it, the hardships, and total experience into a book—along with maps, photos, and material in the back describing the equipment he used.

His book, *Turn Right at Lands End* (Oxford Illustrated Press), has lined up a second marathon for Merrill—this time a long tour of speaking dates to lecture all over England, Scotland, and Wales about his walk to end all walks.

Now whenever others with the itch to go exploring, or with the desire to embark on an adventure, read about Merrill's amazing trip, you can see their eyes light up at the idea of cutting loose on an exploration of their own.

Community Recreation Centers

Wherever you live, chances are good that you probably aren't far from a community recreation center. This is especially true if you live in a fairly large city. These centers offer complete and varied programs of recreation from which you can choose ones that interest you. Some of the activities they offer include the following:

- Game rooms
- Gym classes
- Music classes
- Arts and crafts
- Dances

The mornings at the centers are largely planned for adults, with afternoons for young people who come in after school. A mixture of young people and adults take part in evening programs. Many activities are free, but there may be a small charge for certain programs or classes requiring special instruction.

The city of Memphis operates twenty-five full-time recreation centers (at this writing) for all ages. And they bring a lot of enjoyment to young and older adults.

Recreation at Conventions and Conferences

As an example of the recreation offered during some yearly conventions, The American Booksellers Association has kicked off its last four meetings with a run. Bantam Books, a leading paperback publishing company, sponsors each of these "fun runs," as they are called.

At the last Bantam run, all those participating assembled at 7:05 a.m. at the Peachtree Street entrance to the Hyatt Regency Hotel in Atlanta, Georgia (the site of the last convention). The Atlanta Track Club helped set up the route. Both one-and-a-half and two-mile loops enabled runners to set their own pace and determine how far they wished to run. The yearly run is not a competition, but a record of the finishing times each day is available. Each runner was given a special Bantam ABA Fun-

Run T-shirt and some orange juice. This yearly convention run is quite popular.

Most of the larger conventions and conferences, held in major cities and resort areas, offer a variety of recreation. So don't rule out this recreation option. Whenever you consider attending a convention or conference, find out what kind of recreation is offered.

Fraternity, Sorority, or Club Membership Recreation

College fraternities and sororities have a lot of recreational events during the academic year. These events range from weekend outings, float preparation for homecoming football parades (which can be very competitive), dances, picnics, or competitive sports activities for members, or between other fraternities and sororities.

Even those who graduated years ago are often welcome at many such fraternal events. If you live near a college or university, you have a wide choice of recreation opportunities open to you—from fraternity-sorority events to gym facilities and other college-related activities.

Taking City Tours is Recreational, Informative and Entertaining

I still remember the Gray Line tour I took in Denver, Colorado, a few years ago. Special tour buses took us past clusters of beautiful homes at the foot of the mountains and then on to Lookout Mountain to see the home of Buffalo Bill and the museum there in his honor.

From there we stopped at a number of cliff top sites to catch the unique view of Denver far below and in the distance. It was quite a sight.

Next on the program was a visit to a town nestled right in the mountains. We were given time to get off the bus and look around the area.

On the way back to Denver, the bus stopped at one of the largest mountain amphitheaters in the country. Music concerts are held there regularly. We explored the theater with great interest and again could only marvel at the incredible view of Denver lying far below us in the distance.

All in all, it was one of the best city tours I've taken. I have also enjoyed other tours of Disneyland, Chicago, Toronto, and Montreal. I urge you not to miss these tour opportunities whenever your plans call for travel to large and interesting cities.

Flea Markets Provide Recreation

People with an interest in antiques especially enjoy spending a Saturday or Sunday (or both) at flea markets. They go to them to check the prices and to find any treasures that might turn up. Many varied treasures are found in glass, china, and artwork.

Flea markets are for everyone else too. You don't have to be especially interested in antiques in order to enjoy seeing what is for sale, at what prices, and compared to other items. It's lots of fun to see many posters, buttons, books, furniture, and all manner of items from the past. There are things to be seen at flea markets that appeal to young people and older adults as well. One flea market held in Indiana is so large, according to the reports I get, that people come to it from five surrounding states.

Backpacking

Maybe backpacking is the recreation for you. I'll never forget what four backpackers told me during my last visit to the Grand Canyon. I was standing there at the rim of the canyon, amazed at the sight of it (as I always am). I got to talking to these backpackers about the canyon and its mysteries. They were coordinating their equipment and checking that it was all working okay. They were about to leave (some by burro) for the bottom of the canyon. They planned to spend several nights at the lowest point of the canyon and also near the Colorado River, which looked like a still picture post card from the top of the canyon.

I was struck by their enthusiasm for backpacking. As one of them put it, "There's nothing like backpacking. It's unique. All of us are excited about getting to the bottom of the canyon and surviving down there by the Colorado River on our own."

Rent an Island Villa for the Summer

Back in my navy days, I remember when our cruiser was in Majorca, Spain during February. A group of us from the ship spent most of the free day we had wandering around the fascinating island. Arriving at the top of a hill about noon, which was the highest point on the island, we saw an Englishman out for a stroll with his cane.

He greeted us as he reached the top of the hill. We chatted for a few minutes, while admiring the view. He then told us that he and his wife had been at Majorca for eight months. They had rented an entire villa for an unheard of low price (at that time). A maid came in each day to cook all the meals and do the cleaning and other chores, all for next to nothing in pay.

The Englishman smiled, as he described their life: "I can't get my wife to leave this place. We may be here for life. It's a dream, an adventure we planned, and have fulfilled, but I miss old friends back in England."

Whether you keep your choice of recreation well within the bounds of the traditional types, or decide on something different or even perhaps a bit more dangerous, daring, and adventurous, by all means keep some time in your routine for recreation. By spicing your life with more recreational outlets, you'll enjoy life more and no doubt be a lot healthier for it too. Dr. Caprio and I highly recommend plenty of recreation in your routine.

If you don't have enough recreation in your life at present, refer back to this chapter and look at the other forms of recreation available to you as well. Another code word for enjoyment is recreation. You're bound to thrive on more of it in your life.

17

How to Enjoy a Library

"Stop the grind, I want to get off" is the cry of millions of people every day. And one of the very best places of all to turn off the daily grind is your local library.

"Reading is to the mind what exercise is to the body," said Sir Richard Steele, British dramatist. But reading not only keeps the mind limbered, it soothes the disposition, satisfies the curiosity, and relaxes the troubled spirit. Regardless of the condition of your bankbook, if you can read, you're rich.

Your personal or local library can lift your spirits, make you forget worries, inspire you to imagine, and entertain you. A library literally has the power to change your life, for it can arouse your curiosity and lead you to greater success, satisfaction, and happiness.

"Man does not live by bread alone, but by faith, by admiration and by sympathy," said Emerson. A good library with all its avenues of knowledge and learning stimulates and develops your faith, admiration, and sympathy.

The library can keep you from being lonely. Young people especially are offered marvelous opportunities through the library's services. If teachers truly challenge and stimulate their students, a whole new world of people, places, ideas, and things opens up before a student. And he or she learns that a library can indeed be a pleasant and fascinating place.

118

LIBRARIES HOLD THE WISDOM OF THE AGES

As Hawthorne Daniel says in his book about the National Library Services Act, "The greatest treasures of the modern world are to be found in books. All the accumulated knowledge of mankind—all the wisdom of the ages—all the fables, fantasies, and facts that have interested and delighted the minds of men and women since civilization first began, are available for your pleasure and profit in the books that line the bookshelves of the world."

Amazing as it seems, those who were able to read, until little more than a century ago, were few indeed. It wasn't until after 1776 that public education in America gained greater acceptance. Libraries in the colonial period were private and few. Salisbury, Connecticut was the first town in America to actively support a local library (1810). Others hold that the first town supported (by public taxes and local control) public library was in Peterborough, New Hampshire, in 1833.

From this slow development, there are libraries today in almost every town and city across the country—most of them well-planned and staffed. Many of these libraries are modern, well-designed buildings with highly skilled employees.

THE LIBRARY OF CONGRESS: THE LAST WORD IN LIBRARIES

The Library of Congress, in Washington, is of course the world's largest library. It includes 270 miles of shelves, the early page printed from hand-carved wood blocks, the page printed from the Western World's first printing press, the letters of great men and women who recorded their thoughts on paper, and other photographs, films, and tapes—all preserved for scholars.

In 1815, Thomas Jefferson's personal library of 6,487 volumes was bought by the United States government for $23,950. This purchase doubled the library's size. Today, the main reading room's alcoves contain 25,000 reference books.

Statues of Shakespeare, Beethoven, and other immortals from the past look down on the famous main reading room.

A rare book division includes over 300,000 books, pamphlets, broadsides, and related objects. This division now administers the Houdini and Hitler libraries, along with those of United States presidents. In a typical year, more than 5,000 rare books are cleaned and repaired.

This great Library of Congress constantly adds more information about new leaders, new countries, and new developments in all fields of knowledge. Over the last ten years, about a million old and new items have been added each year.

A day or a week spent at the Library of Congress is an enjoyable and unforgettable experience that merely whets your reading appetite to return again and again. With knowledge more than doubling every ten years, Library of Congress visitors get a vivid example of how much there is to learn about thousands of subjects.

YOUR OWN LOCAL LIBRARY CAN SERVE YOU WELL

You don't have to travel to Washington, D.C. to explore a fascinating world of information and adventure. Your own local library awaits you daily. Browse through the new book section, or head for one of the shelves devoted to a subject of special interest to you. A wide choice of reading and exploration is yours with each new visit. The librarians can be most helpful in locating books of interest to you.

Take a look at the following specific things that your library, and reading, itself, can do for you:

Reading Can Keep Before You the Vision of the Ideal

Making friends with the great and noble thoughts and ideas of the past can strengthen you and assure you that honesty, sincerity, truth, and the rest still count.

Your Library Is a Source of Guidance

Your local library can also guide you individually, should you be thinking of planning a vacation, making an investment, or doing some research on a particular subject. Most libraries subscribe to an incredible number of magazines and newspapers on almost any subject you can think of from astronomy to personal health care, from ballet to zoology.

Libraries Increase Your Understanding

Spending more time in your library can give you a better understanding of human nature. Books and newspapers abound on how to deal effectively with people. You can become a better leader, or supervisor, by reading such material. Also, in many novels and short stories, you can see how people faced and solved various problems. Such knowledge can help you or members of your family.

Today's Modern Library Is a Time Machine

There are magic carpet benefits waiting for you in your library. You can travel the world and never leave your library. Whatever your choice, there is ample material available for you. "Literature is full of perfumes," said Walt Whitman. Your life can be enriched beyond your expectations, if you will see the fantastic opportunities for growth and entertainment and enjoyment open to you with a library card. You can walk with kings, share the lives and adventures of great minds, and even become an expert, yourself, in one or more of a wide variety of fields.

Incredibly Interesting Things Can Be Discovered in Libraries

Many libraries house collections of art reproductions and sculptures that you can borrow for enjoyment in your home. They usually possess large collections of records and tapes which you may borrow. Some even loan tape recorders. They offer recorded courses in learning a foreign language, fascinating recordings on recent history, and many other subjects. Many libraries maintain microform collections of rare books, old newspapers, and other unusual publications that can be yours to discover and enjoy merely for the asking.

Your Library Can Introduce You to Fabulous People

You hear a lot these days about loneliness and how many people in various countries are desperately lonely. If these people only knew how many friends they have waiting in their local library. Marco Polo, Shakespeare, Chopin, Helen Keller, Beethoven, George Sand, Marie and Pierre Curie, General George Patton, Houdini, and on down a long list of some of the most fascinating people of the ages—all await you in your library through the magic of reading. Nobody who can read need ever be lonely.

Think of it. You can live the lives of these amazing people from bygone eras, share their problems, realize their hopes and dreams, and are there with them during the critical and crucial times of their lives . . . all through the portals of biography.

One Simple Question Can Lead You to Fresh Discovery

A few years ago, I was wondering one day how the art of boxing came to be and who actually was the first to box or to really get the sport started. I found the answers I wanted in my local library, in the most interesting story of James Corbett, better known in the boxing hall of fame as "Gentleman Jim."

I learned, for example, that James Corbett was the first heavyweight in history to depend on his boxing skill and not sheer brute strength. I learned how he introduced the art of boxing to the rough-and-tumble brawls of the old days.

Libraries Prove How Much More There Is to Learn

The amount of knowledge today is more than doubling every ten years. As the coming years unfold, this rate of accumulating knowledge will grow even faster. The amount of unexplored knowledge that lies before mankind is staggering. Compare this vast knowledge with the shortness of each of our lives on earth, and the ratio is virtually ironic. There's so much to learn, and yet so little time to learn it.

Using the huge 200-inch telescope on Mount Palomar, scientists are able to see over a billion light-years into space and almost a billion galaxies. Some idea of this incredible distance can be grasped when you realize that a light-year means the distance light travels in a year at 186,000 miles a second.

According to John Cothran, mathematician and chemist, "A photograph of the heavens taken today shows the way the stars looked when the light left them, perhaps millions of years ago."

Space is just one field of knowledge. Add to it all the others, and you get a good idea of the growth possibilities in the years to come.

The truth is that there's so much more to learn and discover . . . that mankind is like a small child standing on a beach looking out to sea. With each visit to a good library, and a glance at all the books, research sources, and periodicals, this thought hits home. Even scholars and others who devote their entire lives to learning admit that they've hardly scratched the surface.

Your Library Can Help You Be Happier Now

Discovering the fun and pleasure of your library can open up a bright new world for you. Your library can very definitely make you a happier person, for the enjoyment it can bring you comes from within and lasts. Think of the stories, articles, novels, and adventures now waiting for you in any large library.

There's no doubt that your library can help you to get more out of each day, even if you don't think that you would like to read that much. In time, you can grow to like reading far more than you might suspect. Millions of people everywhere get up an hour or two earlier (or stay up later at night) so they can keep up with the reading they enjoy and want to do. In the years to come, more free time to do what you wish will become increasingly valuable. To spend a large portion of that time in reading will bring you more enjoyment.

Back in the 1930s and 1940s, fiction was the reading rage.

People at that time wanted to read stories and imaginative material. They still do, but a far greater number of people evidently prefer to read nonfiction, or true material that can help them in their everyday lives.

Libraries Often Show Excellent Films

Many libraries in large cities frequently show any number of fine films. These films are practically always free. You can watch your local newspaper for the announcement of such films. This is one of the few remaining forms of entertainment for the public that is still free. Most of the films shown are classics on the lives of famous people, or travel type films. or occasionally popular movies from yesteryear.

Your Library Can Help You Develop a Hobby

An interesting hobby is a wonderful thing to have. Hobbies enable people to enjoy themselves and to get their minds off their problems and the troubles of the day. Can you imagine going through life without some type of hobby? Many do just that. If you don't now have a hobby, your library can be of real help in suggesting things you might wish to follow as a possible hobby.

If you do have a hobby at present, you can learn far more about it in your local library. Remember the famous birdman of Alcatraz? When one of his pet birds got sick one day, he started reading up on bird diseases and eventually became a world expert and authority on the diseases of birds.

Libraries Are Great Places to Think

Be sure to also keep in mind that a library is a fine place to collect your thoughts, do some serious thinking, study material, and to generally calm down. An Atlanta advertising executive heads straight for the library, whenever he starts feeling uptight, or overloaded with pressures. Within an hour or so in the library, he is able to quiet down, think things out, and get himself back on the job.

Libraries Make Learning
Fun and Enjoyable

Thomas Jefferson strongly believed that learning should be a lifetime pursuit. He proved it in his own life and often had his meals sent to him in his own home library. He just couldn't leave his library. Books, learning, and his own library, which he built over the years, were absorbing interests all his life.

With more frequent visits to your own library, I'm sure you will discover, like many others, that libraries can entertain you as much or more than films, television, or walking the dog.

ENJOY YOURSELF IN YOUR LIBRARY

Remember. Just by finding the right shelf, you can be transported to the Salem witch trials of 1692, or to the last stand at the Alamo, or find yourself aboard the sinking Titanic on that vivid night to remember. Whatever has happened in history, you can be there front row center. You can also experience snow blindness in the Yukon, be imprisoned on Devil's Island, walk the plank for notorious pirates, build your own dream world on your own island, fight in your choice of wars, never grow old in Shangri-la, gamble while riding a Mississippi showboat, and take your pick of thousands of other adventures.

Charles Laughton, the British actor, knew the rich value of reading. In the foreword to one of his books, he wrote: "When I go into a good bookstore or a library, I often feel sad when I see the shelves of books of all kinds that I know I will never be able to enjoy. I think of all the wonderful tales that I will never know, and I wish I could live to be a thousand years old."

So remember. There's always a place where you can turn off the daily grind, unwind, and enjoy yourself. Your local library is a magic carpet. Take advantage of it, and a whole world of enjoyment will be yours over the coming years.

18

Vary Your Daily Routine

Some researchers who have studied the effect of sameness in the lives of various people agree that sanity can be lost by never changing your daily routine.

Monotony does have a disturbing effect on people. There have been many news stories and comments by political leaders on the great monotony in the lives of most assembly line workers. But the truth is that monotony affects us all. "The sameness of people's lives generates boredom that can affect every class of worker—from an advertising executive to a street sweeper," warns Dr. Thomas Myers.

HOW TO VARY YOUR DAILY ROUTINE

Granted that you may well need some changes in your daily routine, here are some suggestions that have worked well for a number of others:

- Go to work a different way. This will help to keep you both sane and happy. There's no rule that says you must go the same way to work every day. Get a map, if necessary, and plan some alternate routes to your office, plant, building, store, school, or wherever you work or must be for the day.

- Think ahead and see what you can plan that will be different for tomorrow or next week. As an example, a college professor friend and I meet some afternoons (when we can get away) and just take a nice half-hour or hour-long walk. Sometimes we walk near the park in the center of our town. Other times we walk on a college campus or in a residential district. The idea is to vary our routine for that day.

There are other ways to do this too. Spend an hour one day next week at an art gallery. Drive by your old school some day, on your way to work. I like to stop by the large student center of one of the colleges in my city. I wander around, browse over the new books and magazines, read some of the funny greeting cards, and often end up upstairs in the snack section for a lemonade or coca-cola. It's not so much what I do as it is the act of doing something different.

- Go see someone. Drop in on an old friend who lives on the other side of town. Look up some of your old school chums, if they're still in town. Perhaps you know of some shut-in who would love to be visited.

- Come back home a new way from the office, or wherever you work. If you can vary the way you go in the morning, you can also do the same thing in the evening.

- Arrange to have *breakfast* with a few associates, colleagues, friends, or neighbors. You could do this at least a few times each week. One top selling insurance agent plans three breakfast appointments each week with prospects. He sells most of them on buying a particular policy. He claims that his breakfast appointments have been an enormous help to his business and also added some needed variety to his daily routine.

- Plan a completely different meal for lunch and at a new place. If you usually eat in a cafeteria, for example, you might go to a restaurant where you could order from the menu direct.

- For different things to do in the evening, in case your usual routine is to watch television, try playing records, working at a picture puzzle, putting on a puppet show with the family, play a game of chess, read a new book, have a "community sing" around the piano with friends and family, play cards, or Monopoly (just to name a few possibilities).

- Many people find it stimulating to spend several evenings a week thinking about their investment program and how they might add to it or make it a more effective one. This isn't work, if you should find it interesting to read over business reports and decide how you can increase your profits. Many find it very fascinating.

    • Find something you would like to collect. As stated earlier, the collecting habit can become enormously engrossing. Edward G. Robinson once described how art collecting can get into the soul of an art lover: "The collecting habit becomes like the drug habit; you cannot live without it. Your walls may be bulging with paintings, business may be bad and prospects none too good, baby needs a pair of shoes, and you've sworn off buying. But honest, it's just this once and there's nothing you can do about it. There's no cure for it. Fact is, you don't want to be cured." Edward G. loved to walk around and look at his pictures. He did it every night. Artists who wrote him often wanted more than just to see his collection: "They would write me, saying they were starving to see some good pictures, and could they see mine? I'd ask them over and they would bring their own pictures along to sell me." Robinson's picture collection brought him great relaxation from his acting work during the day. As he often said, "After a strenuous day at the studio, I find my pictures relaxing. It's like looking through so many windows on a world that is always serene and glowing."

    • Still another way to get some variety in your day is to get up at a different time than you're accustomed to and also go to bed at a different hour.

    • Both Dr. Caprio and I believe that some type of creative work can help you vary your routine. This can be done on a daily basis or perhaps several times a week at least. Hughes Mearns, professor and teacher of creative arts, hits the bullseye when he says that "a gift exists in each of us, some sort of gift; but we must find it for ourselves. The creative spirit is something more than a product in clay and canvas; it is dancing, rhythmic living, a laugh, a flash of the mind, strength of control, swiftness of action, an unwritten poem or story, a song without words; it is life adding its invisible cells to more and more abundant life."

    You can definitely get more enjoyment into your life, if you will vary your daily routine. Follow some of the suggestions in this chapter, or think of others that may be more to your liking. You can come up with some interesting ways to get more variety in your routine, because you know your own routine better than anyone else. Look for ways to add newness to your schedule.

If you've been sticking much too closely to a monotonous routine, start this very week or tomorrow to get some fresh variety into it. It will certainly help you to relax more and get more satisfaction from each day. Your health and sanity deserve this variety, and they will thrive on it. We want you to be around a lot longer. So go for more variety in your daily schedule. You'll like it far better.

19

How American Presidents Have Enjoyed Life . . . Plus Some Unusual Suggestions

Most American presidents have been glad to unwind, to relax and relieve their tensions. They have no choice really. If they don't take time to get their minds off so many problems, the presidency can and will kill them or burn them out.

George Washington followed many recreational interests, including racing, playgoing, cock-fighting, gambling, and dancing. He loved to dance. Even at age fifty, he could dance for hours without stopping.

Gambling was Andrew Jackson's main recreation and outside interest. He liked gambling in all its forms. He owned a racetrack at one time. Even while in the White House, Jackson kept race horses (using the White House stables) and ran them at nearby tracks.

Perhaps remembered more as a statesman and military hero than a farmer, Andy Jackson still depended very much on good crops every year. His main vocation was Tennessee farmer and stock-breeder. He enjoyed showing his crops, barns, and stables to visitors.

Even his gambling and horse-racing interests couldn't relieve Jackson of his worries about his crops. When his days in the White House ended, he remarked: "The rest of my life is retirement and ease." But that first year he was back at the Hermitage (his home in Nashville), a late spring dalayed the germination of the cotton seed. He worried that summer about the results of his cotton crop. Nashville then was a most significant cotton market, and cotton was definitely the money crop.

Unlike most of the other presidents, John Adams didn't have a real hobby. But this did not prevent him from living to be the oldest of all. His son, John Quincy Adams, swam in the Potomac River nude and enjoyed playing billiards. John Quincy Adams kept a diary all his life, and it has proved to be an invaluable historic source.

The president who takes first prize for the most enthusiasm of all has to be Teddy Roosevelt. Teddy's energy supply seemed to come from some vast invisible reservoir. Teddy played tennis with gusto, hunted bears, and thrived on taking Washington officials and other dignitaries on long hikes. Teddy took twenty-mile hikes at the drop of a hat.

Riding, rowing, and bird watching were all loved by Teddy Roosevelt. Despite his busy schedule, he found time for all of them. He was one of America's most stylish and zestful presidents.

Woodrow Wilson was a dedicated golfer through and through. When winter snows turned the White House lawn to white, Wilson used colored golf balls so he could keep hitting them. His average score was about 115. He once coined a vivid description of the game of golf: "An ineffectual attempt to put an elusive ball into an obscure hole with implements ill-adapted to the purpose." Wilson was also a keen fan of vaudeville and was in the audience regularly.

Franklin Roosevelt was a big golfer, too, until polio ended his golfing days. He also liked deep-sea fishing, model ship building, and sailing. Practical jokes gave him great pleasure, and he was constantly playing them, or working out clever new ones, to use on his friends. He also maintained a valuable stamp collection and swam whenever he could find time.

Harry Truman's practice of an early morning walk is of course well-known. Long after he had left the White House, Truman continued this morning ritual for many years. He once said that "when the legs go, it isn't long before the rest goes." He also loved the game of poker and had the great pleasure of once playing the game with Winston Churchill, when the great British leader was visiting in Missouri with Truman.

In addition to a lot of fishing, Calvin Coolidge used a

mechanical horse for much of his exercise. When out on a fishing trip, he wore gloves. Agents who were with him baited the hook and took whatever he caught from the line. Coolidge also enjoyed pitching hay.

President William Howard Taft had an unusual form of relaxation. He was wild about sentimental drama. Sometimes, in the middle of a moving play, Taft would start to cry. Other times he would begin to cry at the end of an especially forceful play. For years, Taft got up at 7:00 a.m. and worked out in his bedroom. He was also a golfer, but his score wasn't too good.

Eisenhower played football at West Point, until a knee injury forced him to stop playing the game. He was very sports-minded. Golf was his favorite, but he was also a good fisherman and an excellent marksman with both pistol and shotgun. He liked to paint, too. Sometimes, while painting, he wouldn't talk to anyone. He derived pleasure also from movies, bridge, cooking, and western reading.

UNUSUAL WAYS TO DEAL WITH TENSION

Along with the traditional ways to relieve tension, which a number of United States presidents followed, here are some additional, unusual methods for beating pressure, stress, and tension: Dr. Caprio and I think you would find them helpful.

1. Spend a part of the summer (or all of it) at an amusement park. One Ohio man who didn't like to go on vacations spent a summer working at a nearby amusement park. He worked for a minimum wage. He found the experience mentally and physically stimulating. If you couldn't spend a long period at such a park, maybe a week or two as a volunteer guide would help to relieve any tension that is bothering you. You would be amply repaid by the smiles of happy visitors and the laughter of children.

2. Set up and operate a concession at local sports events. This is active and often profitable work.

3. Spend your vacation time working as a volunteer at a nature center or wildlife sanctuary. This can be very refreshing. It is also a fine way to lose weight and get a tan, as some who have tried it will admit.

4. If you have any musical ability at all, consider the idea of forming a group. Three school teachers who lost their jobs recently
in the Mid-south area formed a trio and are now being booked
in leading hotel lounges. As they put it, "We receive a lot more
money for a lot less time." Music is of course a wonderful
soother of tension.

5. Spend some time visiting on a dairy farm. The quiet, space, and
routine on a farm can do wonders for any tense feelings you
may have. Farm life, even a short amount of it, can renew your
spirit.

20

Tune in to a
Pleasure Consciousness

Pleasure is an important aspect of your total happiness. It is an antidote for pain. Pleasure should be part of your life, not the whole of it. When you enjoy yourself, life with its painful realities becomes more endurable. To deny that which is normally pleasurable is unintelligent. This does not imply that you should live for pleasure alone.

Strive to adopt a lifestyle that is both meaningful and enjoyable. Become pleasure-conscious. No longer eat to stay alive; eat also for the pleasure of eating. Cohabit for the pleasure release of sexual tension—for the enjoyment of the sex act. The right to enjoy yourself in pursuit of happiness is God-given, not man-made. No one needs to apologize for desiring to be happy, for experiencing better health and for achieving successful fulfillment.

Let's take a quick look at your pleasures. What is it that you do enjoy? Do you like to sing? Then sing. Do you like to dance? Then dance. Ever want to learn to cha-cha or do the twist? Where is the harm? Perhaps you have always thought you would like to take up a hobby like painting. Why not give it a try? It is very relaxing and creative. Maybe you won't be a Rembrandt, but if you are enjoying yourself, why not paint to your heart's content? Get interested in something. Make your life interesting. Develop a healthier and enjoyable philosophy of life.

A Case Illustration of Enjoying Life

When Dr. Caprio asked a thirty-year-old woman to describe in writing what she considered self-fulfilling, she wrote the following:

"To be and yet always to become, to grow and realize myself to the fullest of my capabilities. To have a rock-like integrity and individuality, an inner serenity and strength that is a light to myself and to others. To be able to give to others. To be able to show the human heart and the beauty and mystery of the world, to awaken one soul, as I have been awakened. This is the debt I owe to life, and if I can accomplish this I will have made the world and my life meaningful. I have an insatiable hunger for truth, knowledge, and beauty."

HOW TO MAKE LIFE ENJOYABLE AND PLEASURABLE

One way to *enjoy* life and counteract the painful realities of day-to-day living (to balance the pain-pleasure equation of our existence, as it were) is to explore and exploit the opportunities that arise to enjoy pleasure for pleasure's sake.

Too many of us sabotage our own happiness and enjoyment of life, because of what can be referred to as the guilt syndrome. We were brought up to feel that it is wrong to enjoy ourselves (a forbidden luxury), which is a carryover from our Puritan heritage.

Although we are gradually emancipating ourselves from outmoded taboos, residuals of fanaticism still exist. A certain group of do-gooders, for example, decided recently to ban all rock and roll music because they consider it to be the instrument of Satan and recommended that all music of this kind should be burned. Teenagers were asked to throw all the record albums they enjoyed into one large fire at a public gathering. What could be more irrational?

Fortunately, most of us feel we have the right to find happiness here on earth. It was gratifying to read in a Sunday paper an announcement of a sermon by a local clergyman. He chose for his subject "Why Wait for Heaven to Be Happy?"

It was also comforting to encounter an article like "Pleasure: How to Let Your Senses Rip" by Michael Korda, recently published in *Self* magazine. The writer informs his readers this way: "Pleasure is natural, healthy, necessary. It requires no apology." His thinking obviously coincides with the message of this book on *How to Enjoy Yourself: The Antidote Book for Unhappiness and Depression.*

That pleasure-seeking is a necessity for survival is evidenced by Korda's recommendations: "The best prescription for anything that is wrong with you—boredom, anxiety, not enough money, whatever—is simply pleasure. It isn't a permanent cure, but it's better than drugs, tranquilizers, chain-smoking, coffee or feeling sorry for yourself. The side effects are minimal, the health risks nil, and once you get used to the idea that pleasure, now in the present is good for you, you may stop putting it off and start finding that life is more pleasant. Things are seldom as bad as they seem to be, and pleasure reminds us that life has its sweetness and its compensations."

Korda goes on to add: "The ability to enjoy pleasure for its own sake, without fear or guilt, does not necessarily preclude an ability to deal with the harsher realities of life. There is no point in working hard, for yourself, or for others in business or in politics, if you don't stop to enjoy yourself."

"Educating yourself to pleasure is an important part of life, which is simply to say that you have to be in touch with your own feelings about what makes you happy, and accept them without guilt."

The authors of this book agree wholeheartedly with Mr. Korda. He reenforces the wisdom of Oliver Wendell Holmes: "Life is to be enjoyed."

The Personality Makeup of "Bon Vivants"

There are certain common characteristics of persons (both women and men) who appreciate the "good life." The French refer to them as *bon vivants*, which means people who have *joie de vivre*—who know how to live.

Are bon vivants born that way? Not exactly. They have cultivated the art of enjoying anything and everything—food, sex, people, traveling, prosperity, hobbies, sports—you name it. They are interested in everything that life offers. Because they are acutely aware that life is short ("It's later than you think"), they make every day count. They live every day as though it were their last. We've all seen signs in restaurants and cafes such as "eat, drink, and be merry for tomorrow we die." Is such a philosophy of self-indulgence normal? Why not—provided the enjoyment of pleasure doesn't hurt others, or indulging oneself is not done at the cost of shirking their responsibilities.

Individuals who are able to enjoy life, who are predominantly happy (hedonists) need not apologize for their way of life. They are wiser and better off than the "ascetics" who feel it is sinful to enjoy pleasures. There can be no fun in asceticism. It is based on neurotic self-denial—martyrdom.

The bon vivants have a live-and-let-live attitude. They make friends easily, smile more, are generous and contribute toward making others happy. They take pride in a sense of humor. They appreciate gourmet food and are willing to try anything (within reason, of course) for the first time, whether it's their first roller-coaster ride or their first flight. They are aggressive. They like to experiment. They have a wide range of pleasurable interests including reading, listening to good music, making new friends, participating in sports, cultivating absorbing hobbies, visiting foreign lands, and so on down a long line. They generally dress attractively, are interesting conversationalists, are able to establish rapport with almost anyone they meet. They are free of prejudices. They are not chronic complainers. They are easy to get along with, make good parents, good citizens in their community. They are predominantly givers and not takers. They're altruistic and not self-centered. To put it briefly, these are the wonderful people.

Dr. Caprio believes that if we had more bon vivants in this world, people who have mastered the art of happiness and are able to enjoy life despite its imperfections, we would have fewer divorces, less crime and a better world for all of us to live in.

The ills of mankind arise from unhappiness. Happiness does not breed hatred. To be happy, to enjoy life, to enjoy yourself is God-given. We all have the capacity to participate in life's

pleasures. It only requires self-motivation. We must *want* to enjoy life before it becomes a reality. Seek pleasures and you will
find them.

It is commendable to want to work hard and prosper—to
contribute something worthwhile in your chosen vocation or
career, but it's just as commendable to make your life span
pleasurable. Pleasure neutralizes pain. It makes life more endurable. So why not enjoy . . . enjoy? And, when you discover how to
make yourself happy, share it with others.

21

A Sideline Interest
Can Recharge
Your Batteries

A great many persons these days are getting a lot more enjoyment out of their time, by deciding on a sideline interest, or business, and developing it. It makes sense. A sideline interest gives you something different to challenge your abilities. It adds variety and contrast to your regular routine. And it can certainly stimulate your attitude and renew your vigor. Above all, many such interests bring enjoyment.

In fact, some persons who start a sideline may become more interested in it than in their main line of endeavor. A young lady in Memphis began a "belligram" business about a year ago, mostly for the sheer fun of it. The "belligram" is a Middle Eastern belly dance delivered in the style of a singing telegram. The originator of this new business charged for the service. Today Kareen Luri-Lamm's business has grown by leaps and bounds. Her company is now incorporated. She employs thirteen full-time people, has a studio in Memphis, and is in the process of opening belligram offices in Nashville and Knoxville. The Associated Press did a story on her, and she has been on several network television shows.

Some 4,000 belligrams have been performed at this writing. "I'm having a wonderful time," says Kareen. "We must be doing something right. I'm making money, but I'm also putting a lot back into the company because we have stage productions that need costumes, and I provide them."

The point is that Kareen was enjoying herself, and her

new business, before it began to skyrocket. The whole thing started as a fun project for her.

The Woman Who Originated "Meet the Press"

Martha Rountree is founder and president of Leadership Foundation of Washington. The purpose of the organization is "to set up lines of communication from Washington to the grassroots. We are interested in many issues—national defense, violence on television, prayers in the schools—but our job is not to make decisions, but to provide the facts, the pros and cons, of the issues so the people can make the decisions."

Before Miss Rountree introduced "Meet the Press" to Washington, in 1950, politicians refused to be on radio or television without previously prepared speeches. But Martha Rountree persuaded them to go on the air without such scripts.

Part-Time Laborer to Millionaire

Gregory Edwards started his sideline interest at the tender age of ten. He began studying the stock market. By age twelve, he was making investments on paper. He had invested $40 in stocks at sixteen. Today Edwards is a millionaire.

Edwards worked his way through high school in a florist shop and earned $50 a week. By eighteen, he was getting $3.02 an hour as a part-time laborer for a meat-packing plant (while still in school).

As Edwards sums up his achievements, "It's a challenge to me to get into a field that has been alien to me and really make a go of it. It's my way of saying that winning is great—you can't knock winning—but even greater to me is playing the game. We are living in the most exciting time in the history of the world."

DETERMINING THE SIDELINE INTEREST OR BUSINESS FOR YOU

Once you know you would enjoy having a sideline interest, the next step is to find the right one for you. You will find the following questions helpful, when thinking about possible sidelines:

1. Are you interested in a sideline *interest* or a sideline *business* (in which you can grow and make money)? In other words, some sideline interests won't yield a profit for you. But any number of sideline businesses will make money for you and bring you enjoyment too.

2. When thinking of a possible sideline business, remember this. *Curiosity* is one of the strongest human incentives. People want *bargains* today like never before. People do not want cheapness. There's a difference. Ask yourself this question: What sideline business could I launch to provide people with a bargain? (perhaps a new product or service of some kind)

3. Does your background, training, job experience, special knowledge, or education hold any clues for a sideline interest or business you can start? An engineer in the Midwest, for example, had long been interested in the music business. So he built an elaborate recording studio in his home and now produces commercial records. He is now in the music business (as a sideline) in a professional way and is making money. But he did it for the enjoyment of it. It should also be noted that he had the money and knowledge to plan and build the recording studio in his home.

4. Is there a sideline interest, or business, I would enjoy pursuing and developing . . . possibly over an extended period of time? In other words, don't fool yourself. Don't jump into an involved sideline, unless you believe you would enjoy it over the long haul. Study up on it and do some serious thinking about it. Keep in mind that it's entirely possible to try less involved sidelines, in order to see if you enjoy them.

Suggestions for Sideline Interests

Here are some possible sideline interests you might want to consider. Remember that you have a wide selection to choose from. The ones listed here are just a few possibilities:

- UFO's — This is a fascinating interest for a growing number of people.
- Songwriting — Some twenty million people in America alone are trying to write songs. But many of these songwriters are in it for the enjoyment of creating new lyrics and music.

- Treasure Hunting — Keep in mind that this interest can be an expensive one, especially if it means diving to find a treasure aboard a sunken ship.
- Public Speaking — You speak to local groups, clubs, and organizations. This is a fascinating sideline interest. And it could develop into a full-time career for you.

  Writing — You can write articles and features for magazines and newspapers, or novels, non-fiction books, greeting cards, jokes, television and motion picture scripts, and a variety of other material. Dr. Caprio and I recommend both writing and speaking.
- Modeling — This interest can often fit in with another career. It offers a good chance for growth, regardless of your age.
- Bridge — This popular game brings enjoyment to millions on any given day. Many bridge clubs meet on a regular basis, and bridge tournaments are unforgettable experiences.
- Chess — This game is unique and always a challenge. In addition to the enjoyment of chess, it is also mentally stimulating. Chess clubs have sprung up everywhere in recent years.
- Bowling — I know bowlers who don't chalk up high scores, but they still love the game. It's good exercise and enjoyable to see how many of those pins you can knock down. And it's fun to see if you can improve your score over a period of time, which most bowlers can do.
- Stamp Collecting — People who follow this sideline interest never seem to be bored. They are always after any number of new stamps. And along with the enjoyment of it, it can be a valuable part-time activity. Many stamps have greatly increased in value.

Suggestions for a Sideline Business

Bear in mind that some businesses you may start are more involved, complicated, and expensive (to get launched) than others. So get all the facts first and think well on those of interest to you, before proceeding. The following suggestions are just a few of the many choices you have:

- A Neighborhood Security Business — Some new companies are doing quite well providing a patrol and security service for various sections of large cities. Since the police in major cities can't be everywhere, this business idea is a natural. And it is growing.

- A Seminar Promotion Business — Some seminar promoters are netting over $50,000 for a three-day series.
- Buy and Sell Paperbacks — You would of course need space where customers could come to look over your books. But many of these outlets are small and the rental, or purchase price, may be reasonable.
- Start a Student Tutoring Service — The advantage here would be the fact that you could do this in the evening and on weekends.
- Make and Sell Your Own Homemade Candy — Again, your weekends could be very profitable with such a business. Make the candy during the week and sell it on weekends. Some enterprising couples are netting $500 every weekend in this business of their own.

The above suggestions are just a few to get you thinking about the possibilities of a sideline business or service you might provide. You can contact the Small Business Administration office in your area, or at 1441 L Street, N.W., Washington, D.C. 20416. They can provide you with more information on your specific business interests, or you can check your local library.

Remember. Many people who launch a sideline interest or business eventually make their part-time endeavor a full-time enterprise. But even if it remains just a sideline for you, it will bring you a greater sense of satisfaction, a chance to use more of your talents and abilities, and increased enjoyment over the passing years.

22

Plan Enough Fun-Filled Travel

Travel is more than enjoyable. It's splendiferous! Many view it as a luxury. As you make your plans and build your hopes for the future, be sure that you have enough travel lined up, or in mind, for yourself and those dear to you.

The trend at this writing is for more frequent travel for shorter periods of time. Instead of one long vacation a year, more persons and families are taking off on periodic two- and three-day trips.

Look, for example, at the fun-filled travel I enjoyed last summer because I split it up into separate trips:

- I attended a convention in Atlanta for five days.
- I flew from Atlanta to Fort Lauderdale, Florida, for three more days.
- On June 18, I fiew to Montreal, Canada for five days, followed by three days in New York.

Now look at the advantages you can derive from several trips, for shorter periods of time, rather than a one-, two-, or three-week vacation a year:

1. You have several trips to plan and look forward to instead of only one.

2. You can often combine some of your business with travel. As an example, all of the travel I did last summer (to Atlanta,

Fort Lauderdale, Montreal, New York, and Chicago) was directly related to my work as an author and advertising consultant. This means that part of the expenses of the trips are tax-deductible.

3. You see a variety of sights in several different places. You're not stuck with just one location that a single vacation trip means. As an example, I took the city and harbor tours of Montreal, which included an hour-long visit to Old Montreal, one of the most interesting sights in the city.

4. You aren't away from home (and your job, business, or main line of work) for a long period of time. A two- or three-week trip is a long time to be away (for certain types of businesses or career-related activities). Several short trips (three, four, or five days each) keep you away for much shorter periods of time.

5. It is more enjoyable and exciting to travel to three or more different places than just to one. When returning from one short trip, you know you have others coming up in the near future or whenever.

Half the Fun Is in the Planning

Part and parcel of the joy of travel lies in the planning of it. Here are some good travel suggestions you might want to consider at some time in the future:

• This is one trip I have never gotten to take as yet, due to timing or other conflicts, but I urge you to consider it. Fly, go by train, or drive to Seattle, Washington. Spend a day or two there and then go on to Vancouver, Canada. I've been to Vancouver several times and can recommend this utterly beautiful and interesting city in British Columbia to you with enthusiasm. After several days in Vancouver, take the Alaskan Passage route by ship to Alaska. You will, reportedly, see some of the most gorgeous sights and scenery in the world on your way to Alaska. You can end your trip with, hopefully, a week (or at least several days) in Alaska (and longer if possible).

Now I grant you that this Alaskan trip, if done as suggested, might take as long as two weeks (or more). But if you vary several short trips with a somewhat longer one, as many do, then this Alaska by ship route would make a fine choice. It would be missing a lot to have to leave for home, upon arriving in Alaska. You would want more time to see at least some of this last frontier.

• Another good travel bet is to fly to Montreal, spend a few days there, and then take the train across Canada to either Toronto or all the way to Vancouver. A variation on this idea is to fly to Vancouver, spend several days there, and then catch the train going east to Montreal. The point of this trip is to cross Canada on the comfortable and well-operated trains that cross that great land. You'll see superb scenery. This trip by train across Canada is very popular with families, as well as with individuals. The entire trip could be taken in a short amount of time.

• How about flying to London on one of the seven-day show packages, offered by a number of travel agencies? This package deal, for a flat rate, provides for your hotel, round-trip-air-flight, a number of tickets to current shows in London, and some of your meals. It's a short but enjoyable seven-day trip. If you like plays and stage shows, this travel idea is especially recommended.

• Visit and tour the Black Hills of South Dakota. I urge you to head for South Dakota on one of your future trips. The Black Hills are filled with historic interest. It was considered to be sacred grounds to the Indians in the last century. It makes a delightful trip by car. If you don't wish to drive, a bus is your best bet to see the area. Rapid City, South Dakota is a good place to stay as your headquarters, while seeing the entire area. You can then take day-long side trips to see varous sights in the Black Hills, the Passion Play, which is performed before a packed audience, Mount Rushmore, and those areas where buffalo can still be seen.

• Watch a variety of publications for seven-day cruises (information on them) to interesting places. Sometimes these cruises feature a name entertainer, or music star, for the length of the cruise.

• Eureka Springs, in Arkansas, is a magnet for visitors and travelers. There are activities going on there throughout the year including arts and crafts shows, the great Passion Play most nights, an antique car festival (held usually in September), and a series of events and programs sponsored by any number of clubs, organizations, and groups in the area. This unique little town has attracted nationwide publicity. Land values there have skyrocketed in recent years, and new facilities have been added to offer entertainment and good accommodations. During the 1880s and 1890s, Eureka Springs was a highly popular health spot. Walking or driving through the town is like a trip into the past. For a short or extended vacation, keep this most interesting town in mind.

• Weekend at Shiloh. About 100 miles east of Memphis, Tennessee, is one of the most awesome battlefields of the Civil War—Shiloh National Park. If you ever get close to this area, don't miss seeing it. They have fixed it so you can take a driving tour of Shiloh, without getting out of your car. You'll no doubt want to walk around some too, in order to more closely see the old Shiloh Church, or Meeting House, where the grim battle gets its name, the famous Cherry Mansion (used by Grant for a headquarters), the Union and Confederate battle lines, the trenches, Bloody Pond, Hornet's Nest, and cannons sitting silently in the fields, very near the exact positions they held during the battle.

• Salt Lake City is another fascinating place you might visit. The Mormon Tabernacle Choir (the most famous in the world) will stir you with its unforgettable effect. You can also take the tour of Temple Square and learn a great deal about the Mormons. Many visitors also enjoy seeing the Great Salt Lake.

• Visit the Crater of Diamonds in Murfreesboro, Arkansas. For a small fee, you can spend a delightful afternoon (or entire day) looking for diamonds at this famous site. Many diamonds, small and large, have been found at this mine over the years, and millions of people have made the trip to visit the mine, the museum there showing pictures of the variety of diamonds discovered on the land, and to walk and dig on the grounds in hopes of uncovering still more diamonds. I've been there myself, and I can vouch for the enjoyment I had from just knowing that I was looking for diamonds. I didn't find any during the long afternoon I spent there. But I had a lot of fun.

If you prefer to plan a more unusual type of trip, there are various options open to you. One writer I know has visited the libraries across the country. Another writer researched all the merry-go-rounds in the nation, in order to write her book on the subject.

One trip a friend of mine has long believed would be quite interesting, and also unusual, would be to travel across the country staying in different monasteries, or convents, along the way. Many such monasteries do welcome visitors, provided they don't stay too long.

Wherever you would like to travel, I urge you to put your plans into action. Don't delay time and again, thinking that you will do such travel years from now, or when you get a chance. That time may never come. You must take the time, if necessary, to get in some travel each year. Otherwise, the years will slip by, and you'll wish one day that you had taken the short, or long, trips you once considered.

Interview With a World Traveler

Dr. Frank Caprio, the co-author of this book, is a good example of the enjoyment one can realize from travel. Here are some of the answers Dr. Caprio gave in an interview about travel and the great enjoyment it brings:

Q. *Dr. Caprio, what is one of your greatest pleasures in life?*

A. Travel. In the 1950s, my wife and I took a trip around the world on the *President Monroe*, which was the only ship that went at that time. We were the only couple who completed the trip. It was an absolutely marvelous experience.

Q. *What other world travel have you enjoyed?*

A. We took trips to South America, Scandinavia, and three additional trips to Europe.

Q. *How much, approximately, would you say you have spent on travel over the years?*

A. About $140,000. This travel made me realize that it's a big world. God put one sky over all of us. He meant it to be a world of all kinds of people.

Q. *What else has travel made you realize?*

A. Mainly how insignificant each person is . . . that you're only one leaf on the tree of life.

Q. *Have you known people who were unable to enjoy the travel they did?*

A. Oh, yes. It's better to think that you're going to have a good time on a trip. It's better to think this in advance. I know of a widow who took a trip to the Scandinavian countries, but she could only think, all during her travels, that her husband should have been with her.

Q. *Is there anything else you'd like to add?*

A. Yes. I think many people worry about the hereafter too much. You create your own heaven or hell on earth. Don't wait 'til death to enjoy heaven. God wants us to enjoy life. I think people should buy a car, if they want it . . . take a trip . . . go to Europe. Too many adopt the attitude of thinking this way: "I won't enjoy myself until I go to heaven." I think the purpose of life is to enjoy everything in the here and now.

Along with the pure enjoyment of it, one of the strongest reasons for travel is simply because it's good for your health. Doctors often advise their patients to travel, because they know it relieves the pressures and strains of modern day living that tend to build up sooner or later.

So mark it well in your book of must do's. Get enough fun-filled travel in your life. Decide on where you want to go, make your plans, and put them into action. You'll be glad you did. Remember. "Travel maketh a whole person." And it's also very true that travel maketh a person whole.

23

An Enjoyment
Self-Assessment Test
(Are You Able to
Enjoy Yourself)

1. Do you dislike being around people, feel tired all the time, and complain about being bored?

2. Do you consider yourself difficult to get along with?

3. Are you pessimistic about your chances of becoming happy and successful?

4. Do you neglect your appearance and are indifferent about cleanliness or what you wear?

5. Are you deliberately avoiding friends, preferring to be alone?

6. Are you easily upset over trivial disappointments?

7. Are you overly health conscious—worrying about ailments that are psychosomatic (emotionally induced)?

8. Are you taking life more seriously and enjoying it less?

9. Do you suffer from frequent spells of depression?

10. Are you living more and more in the past?

11. Do you find it difficult to be cheerful, to smile and to relate to people?

12. Are you "hooked" on tranquilizers to carry you through the day?

13. Are you a chronic worrier?

14. Do you feel sorry for yourself or believe that life has passed you by?

15. Do you suffer from a negative self-image?

16. What kind of a person are you?

17. Do you hate yourself?

You cannot hope to establish a healthy relationship with others, as long as you harbor feelings of self-hatred. This is synonymous with self-punishment. You are taking out on yourself the hostility that you have created for your own self.

Self-hatred can become a habit. Counteract the self-hatred with self-acceptance and self-love.

18. Are you too shy?

Self-confidence is the antidote to shyness. Shyness can represent disguised vanity. You are afraid you are not making a good impression, so you become shy. You are thinking about your fear of not being well-received and accepted and loved, and this fear that it may not come about makes you withdraw.

19. Are you overly critical?

Over-criticalness indicates disguised self-displeasure.

20. Do you possess a distorted sense of values?

We are living in a time when emphasis is placed on material things. We are more concerned about being considered successful financially than successful in character. Not that material things are insignificant, but if they have been your major emphasis and you feel unhappy, cheated by life, or as if something is missing, it is a good indication that you need to begin to develop an appreciation for things of the mind.

21. Do you suffer from an inferiority complex?

To have an inferiority complex is understandable, but to remain inferior is unforgivable. And needless. Study something that makes you an expert. Gain confidence by doing.

22. Are you adrift without goals in life?

The saddest people I know are those who have no goals. They seek psychotherapy, saying, "What is there to live for?"

To enjoy yourself, you must have goals. It is one way of getting the greatest amount of self-satisfaction.

23. Are you over-sensitive?

Over-sensitivity is synonymous with excessive self-preservation. You are giving yourself more importance than you deserve. Desensitize yourself and promise yourself that no one can demoralize you or make you lose confidence in yourself.

24. Are you too conceited?

Persons who are conceited are covering up for an inferiority complex. Conceit is the other side of the same coin. It is related to other undesirable traits, such as snobbishness, vanity, aloofness. It is also associated with false pride. A person who has achieved great things has no need to feel conceited. Almost without exception, great people are humble and modest. People who are conceited lose friends rapidly. They make themselves obnoxious.

25. Are you immature?

Most people understand the meaning of immaturity. It implies the traits of a child, who has not learned to control his or her desires, emotions and thinking, selfishness, emotional instability, and lack of wise judgment. A person who is immature wants his way in everything. He or she may be excessively jealous, or give vent to outbursts of temper. He sulks and he pouts.

26. Are you a chronic complainer?

An excessive, or unreasonable, complainer is a person who complains for the sake of complaining. He or she believes everyone is against him. Chronic complainers are unhappy people. They are unable to enjoy themselves.

27. Are you an escapist, running away from responsibility?

Note: Think about your answers to these questions. Decide if these are problems that are keeping you from being happy and enjoying yourself?

24

Checklist for a Joyous Future: 76 Ways to Enjoy Yourself, Starting Today

1. Decide now to make your own happiness . . . and do just that every day.

2. Take the time to do those things you feel are important for you.

3. Cultivate the capacity for change, for it is the key to enjoying your life.

4. Believe that your future will be an enjoyable one. Then try to create a happy one for yourself.

5. Determine some clearly-defined goals and the steps necessary to realize them.

6. Don't let your body rule your mind. Say to yourself every day: "I feel terrific."

7. Use your imagination every day if possible. Take up art, music, literature, poetry, or other creative activity. Being creative (whatever the activity) will keep you happy and feeling good.

8. Take a short break now and then from your work or routine. Such breaks renew your vigor.

9. Turn your problems into stepping-stones that will help you reach your goals.

10. Spend some time regularly with books, ideas, and music. They are mind lifters.

11. Don't wait for a certain time to be happy, or until you

have obtained something you want. Be happy today while you can.

12. Beware of over-extending yourself in your work, for it can lead to job burnout.

13. Enjoy your coffee breaks, lunch hours, and vacations. You deserve them.

14. Strive to discover your true talents and abilities. Then develop them as much as possible.

15. Share the experience of watching a dawn or a sunset with a loved one.

16. Try to save more of your income in the coming years, if at all possible. Look at the current percentage of income saved by the following countries:

West Germans — Save 15 percent of their disposable income
British — Save 13 percent
Japanese — Save a whopping 25 percent
Americans — Save only 5 percent

17. Developing a pleasure-consciousness can be a good antidote for burnout.

18. To remain unhappy indefinitely is abnormal. Chronic unhappiness is an illness of the mind.

19. Love of yourself and of life, itself, is the best antidote for unhappiness.

20. Make each morning when you awake a new beginning—a new opportunity to make each day a good day.

21. Believe that you are capable of being happy and enjoying yourself.

22. Happiness comes from within. It is a learned habit of enjoying not necessarily the big things of life, but all of the little things.

23. Faith in yourself and in a higher power can work miracles of love, happiness, and peace of mind in your life.

24. As Dr. Norman Lunde said, "Life produces for you just what you believe about yourself."

25. You will never be lonely if you show people that you care about them.

26. To achieve a more enjoyable life, start with yourself. Don't expect people or the world to change, to suit your desires and needs. You, yourself, must change.

27. Learn how to relax. It is far easier to enjoy yourself if you know how to relax.

28. Don't live in the past or in the future. Be as happy as you can during each day, as it comes.

29. Lie on a beach next summer and listen to the relentless sound of the surf.

30. Remember the sign at the plantation Scarlett O'Hara visited, in *Gone With the Wind:* "Do not squander time, for that is the stuff life is made of."

31. Fall in love with the joy of learning. Become a continuous learner, for even a lifetime cannot scratch the surface of all the interesting things there are to learn.

32. Smile and the world will smile with you and back at you.

33. The world steps aside for the women or men who know where they're going.

34. Laughter does wonders for you. It is healthy because it increases your heart rate and circulation.

35. Use humor to relieve boredom.

36. Choose a form of exercise you can enjoy. Then exercise that way regularly.

37. Try to realize and appreciate good morale in the work you do.

38. Write little notes, memos, or reminders to yourself that will help you stay organized and do better work.

39. Stay curious about new approaches to your work (or various aspects of it).

40. Project yourself into the future. If you don't feel you'll be happy in the same work (job or profession) years from now, start making plans *now* for a switch to a different field.

41. See yourself continually as *victorious* over the effects of burnout.

42. Learn to think ahead more. It is one of the most valuable tools for happy and successful living.

43. Avoid taking work home with you at night and over weekends. Use your evenings and weekends to relax and enjoy yourself.

44. Listen to the signals of your body. When your body tires, it lets you know it with a variety of clues. Delaying the rest you need may bring on an illness.

45. Vacations help you mentally and physically. They provide you with different sights, activities, and things to think about. Don't skip them.

46. Vary the place where you eat lunch from day to day. This adds interest and variety to your day.

47. Browse for an hour or so in a good bookstore, at least once a month.

48. Whenever you're disappointed about something, flash your mind back to those times and occasions when you were victorious.

49. When loneliness threatens to engulf you, remember that you remain in control. The resources to snap out of loneliness (and the blues) are within you.

50. You can overcome loneliness by keeping busy and active.

51. Sex can be as enjoyable as you want it to be.

52. To dream, to learn, to think, to work and to laugh form a sound philosophy of life.

53. The sex act between a man and a woman can represent the ultimate expression of love.

54. Sexual fulfillment adds to the joy of existence.

55. Promise yourself to look at the sunny side of everything and make your optimism come true.

56. One of the best assurances for enjoyment in your life is the development of one or more hobbies. Start or expand a hobby in which you are genuinely interested.

57. Compliment your marriage mate every day. Everyone likes to feel that he or she is appreciated.

58. Read E.B. White's *Charlotte's Web* aloud to a favorite child.

59. Collecting is a most enjoyable pursuit. Think about

starting your own collection. Some possibilities include dolls, coins, posters, record albums, buttons, books, or whatever may interest you.

60. Take five minutes now and then to daydream about your hopes, interests, goals, and activities.

61. Get and maintain enough recreational outlets in your life.

62. Check the planned recreational programs at community recreation centers found in most large cities. Then take part in those of interest to you.

63. Study how others have found the time to do a lot and achieve a great deal.

64. An impromptu, all-day outing is an excellent way to renew yourself.

65. Take time to play. It is the secret of perpetual youth.

66. Check into the flea markets in your area. They are relaxing, fun, and informative too.

67. Unwind now and then in your local library. Make it your magic carpet to other eras. countries, lifestyles, centuries, and the lives of fascinating people (both real or imagined). Try doing some of your thinking in a library. The quiet atmosphere can be quite helpful.

68. Do something creative each day, even if you only give thirty minutes or so to it.

69. Try cutting the time you spend watching television in half. Use this time to do something different and new.

70. Teach some children a favorite old game—Monopoly, Parcheesi, Clue, or even chess. Or invent a new one.

71. For the sake of variety, get up and go to bed at a different hour than you usually do.

72. Go to work, the office, school, or wherever you have to be each day a different way.

73. Reading can keep before you the vision of the ideal, prevent you from being lonely, and open a whole world of enjoyment to you. If you can read, you are already rich.

74. Make a *list* of the things you enjoy. Then add to your list continually. This increases your pleasure-consciousness. And pleasure neutralizes pain.

75. Spend some time (a weekend or longer) visiting on a farm. The quiet of a farm will reduce tension and renew your spirit.

76. Launch a sideline interest (or business). It can bring you a greater sense of satisfaction and become a real source of enjoyment for you.

Some evidence suggests that people who are unhappy and depressed most of the time for no good reason may have inherited their condition. In such cases, treatment by a physician or psychiatrist with powerful new prescription drugs may give these individuals a measure of happiness they would never have thought possible.

The Enjoyment "Idea Bank"

☐ Sing

If you're not doing any singing, while in your daily shower or bathtub, you're missing a great deal of enjoyment. You may not feel like singing every time you take a shower, but keep in mind that here is where you can sing to your heart's content. It's great fun, it's relaxing, and it's healthy too.

☐ Go to School

Consider enrolling in a night (or summer) course at a local college, university, or public school in your area. Here are some examples of continuing education classes that were offered in a recent year by a major school in the Mid-south area:

- Creative Stitchery
- Bridge
- Real Estate Exam Preparation
- Racquetball
- Basic Photography
- Creative Sewing
- Tennis for Fun
- Class Piano for Children
- Figure Control (exercises designed to help women improve and control their figures)

- Cake Decorating
- Conversational French
- Home Furnishing and Decorating
- Drawing and Sketching
- Learning to Write Poetry
- Wine and Cheese Tasting

☐ Look for Treasure

At some time in the future, the enjoyment of treasure hunting may well appeal to you. There is even romance in this increasingly popular business of treasure hunting for fun and profit.

Mel Fisher is one such treasure seeker who has been trying (at this writing) to find the treasure of a seventeenth-century Spanish galleon. The ship was lost in a hurricane in 1622. Over 300 people went down with the ship.

Fisher's patience in looking for the treasure for some eight years was rewarded. One of his divers found a seven-foot gold chain weighing ten pounds. A six-inch gold bar was also discovered.

The daring, adventure, and continuous appeal of wondering what may be discovered next has added a lot of romance to the fine art of treasure hunting—whether on land or beneath the sea.

☐ Read

To increase your creativity, read more. Read everything you can get your hands on—books, newspapers, poetry, newsletters, bulletins, booklets, or whatever.

Vita Sine Libris Mors Est
(Life Without Books Is Nothing)

If you're not a reader at present, you're only half alive. Become a reader. Make this your project. To establish the reading habit, do two things: (1) Read an article (or other material) each day and then ask yourself what you learned. (2) Before long, you'll find that reading has become a habit.

Reading triggers the imagination and will bring you numerous ideas. Courses in literature will bring you in contact with other readers. Great Books discussion clubs meet in many public libraries.

Hughes Mearns, teacher of creative arts, hits the bullseye when he says that "a gift exists in each one of us, some sort of gift; but we must find it for ourselves."

Romance Novels Bring Enjoyment to Millions

If you aren't reading romance novels already (or general novels and nonfiction on subjects of your choice), you are missing a lot of enjoyable hours.

No less a world figure than the late Anwar Sadat admitted his liking for romance novels: "I always read Barbara Cartland when I have the time."

☐ Visit Disney's Kingdom

A vacation kingdom of infinite extravaganza awaits you in Orlando, Florida. Whether you have a few days, or a week (or longer), a visit to Disney World is an experience you won't forget.

Disney World features a Magic Kingdom theme park, several resort hotels, vast acres of lakes and waterways, two golf courses, and unlimited recreation-entertainment offerings.

☐ Change Your Job

It's been estimated that in the United States alone over 100,000 executives change jobs each year. In a number of job fields, variety in your background may even be an asset.

Changing your job could well be just what you need, in order to get more enjoyment out of life and to feel happier. If you aren't sure what job you would like to switch to, you might consult the *Directory of Approved Counseling Agencies*, published by the American Board on Counseling Services. You'll find a copy of this directory in most public libraries. The directory lists good counseling agencies near you.

What do you need with a counseling agency? Such an agency offers you experienced and capable vocational guidance

—help that could easily lead you into happier and more successful work.

One of the big guidance problems is the incredible variety of ways to earn a living in the world today. The United States Labor Department's *Dictionary of Occupational Titles* lists over 20,000 different jobs.

It's healthy and satisfying to get into the kind of work that you will like and enjoy. According to Dr. Karl Menninger, "Three-fourths of psychiatric patients suffer from dissatisfaction in their work."

Don't, however, leave your present position until you have lined up your next job. The saying is true: "The best time to get a job is when you already have one."

☐ Read the Bible

My grandmother patterned her life on the great wisdom of the Proverbs. A happier and more enjoyable philosophy of life can be built around them. Here is a partial list of some of the proverbs:

- "Strike while the iron is hot."
- "Laugh, and the world laughs with you."
- "All that glitters is not gold."
- "Actions speak louder than words."
- "Who loses honor can lose nothing else."
- "Let not the sun go down upon your wrath."
- "Hitch your wagon to a star."
- "Beauty is a fading flower."
- "There is no education like adversity."
- "Birds of a feather flock together."
- "A fool and his money are soon parted."
- "He loves his country best who strives to make it best."

☐ Join A Club

This may seem like an obvious way to find enjoyment (in and through a club), but think about it awhile. Are you perhaps overlooking a club you might join? Here is a partial list of clubs to consider:

- Country clubs
- Service clubs
- Hobby clubs and groups (camera, bridge, astronomy, chess)
- Professional clubs
- Patriotic clubs
- Sports and recreational clubs
- Travel clubs
- Civic clubs
- Religious and charitable organizations
- Music and art clubs

☐ Audition for a Play

You don't have to be any great shakes of an actor or actress to land a small part in a play. Some plays call for spear carriers, or crowd people, or very small walk-on roles. It's often easier than you might realize to get a role in a hometown or local area production.

The way to try for one is to watch the newspapers. You'll see (often) a notice for auditions—especially in large cities. You have only to show up at the right time, express your interest, and read for the part. It can be a lot of fun just to try out for a role and a most enjoyable experience to appear in a play or musical production. And, volunteers are always needed for backstage and front-office tasks, in every "straw hat" or summer theater. You'll have fun, too.

☐ Start a Business

Here are some ideas of businesses that are doing very well at this writing:

1. Donut shop—Some owners are netting up to $75,000 a year.
2. Pipe shop—This kind of shop is simple and not expensive to set up.
3. Earring shop—Along with earrings, you could also offer ear-piercing.
4. Cake shop—A California woman earned $64,000 in a recent year offering delicious cakes.

5. Health food store—Many of these stores are small, but they are doing well. Some are netting $75,000 and up a year.

6. Find-a-Roommate Service—With so many sharing apartments and homes these days, this business service is currently booming. One company reportedly grossed $60,000 in a recent year offering this service.

☐ Begin a Collection

Starting a collection is a prime source of enjoyment and a continuous one too. Early film star Harold Lloyd collected records and albums and had more than 10,000 of them. It was said by those who knew him that Lloyd could find any one record album of the 10,000 at any time.

Lloyd also loved to create Christmas trees, and he used the garden room of his unique Beverly Hills home for this special purpose. His tree creations became famous. The trees were huge, and he collected ornaments for them constantly. The last tree he put up was a fabulous one with more than 5,000 ornaments on it. It stood over fourteen feet tall and nine feet wide. Many of the beautiful and colorful ornaments were made by friends of Lloyd and his wife.

☐ Enjoy Beauty

Beauty is everywhere. It rises with every dawn and weaves through sunsets; it leaves its calling card in every rainbow; it's there in the white blanket of snow during the middle of winter; it silhouettes the sky as a flock of birds flies homeward; it's there looking up from the eyes of a baby, in the melodic strain of a symphony orchestra, the precision of a ballet, or the thousands of twinkling stars in the late night heavens.